Stefan Collini

Matthew Arnold

A Critical Portrait

CLARENDON PRESS · OXFORD

*This book has been printed digitally and produced in a standard specification
in order to ensure its continuing availability*

OXFORD
UNIVERSITY PRESS

Great Clarendon Street, Oxford OX2 6DP

Oxford University Press is a department of the University of Oxford.
It furthers the University's objective of excellence in research, scholarship,
and education by publishing worldwide in

Oxford New York

Auckland Cape Town Dar es Salaam Hong Kong Karachi
Kuala Lumpur Madrid Melbourne Mexico City Nairobi
New Delhi Shanghai Taipei Toronto
With offices in
Argentina Austria Brazil Chile Czech Republic France Greece
Guatemala Hungary Italy Japan South Korea Poland Portugal
Singapore Switzerland Thailand Turkey Ukraine Vietnam

Oxford is a registered trade mark of Oxford University Press
in the UK and in certain other countries

Published in the United States
by Oxford University Press Inc., New York

ISBN 978-0-19-954188-1

To Ruth

Preface

A short book on a writer as rich and diverse as Matthew Arnold must, more than most books, be highly selective. It therefore seems only fair to alert the reader to the chief idiosyncrasies of the portrait of Arnold I have chosen to offer here. Although I have naturally tried to do justice to the range of his achievement, I have judged (not very controversially) that it is as a literary and social critic that he chiefly commands attention today, and that it is his work in these areas written in the 1860s, above all *Essays in Criticism* and *Culture and Anarchy*, which best exhibits his special gifts. I recognize that others might wish to give greater prominence to his books on religion than I do, and that a stronger case could be made for the importance of the critical essays he wrote in the last decade of his life. More contentiously, where some assessments of Arnold might decide to give pride of place to his poetry, I have felt inclined not only to follow the rough proportions of his *œuvre*, in which the prose bulks far larger than the poetry, but also to let the distribution of the chapters reflect my conviction that, for reasons to do with our own cultural preoccupations as much as with the merits of his writing, the best of his prose has a claim on us today that cannot be matched by his poetry.

If the result of giving greater prominence to his writings of the 1860s has been to create a more winning and cheerful Arnold than might naturally issue from concentrating on the poetry or the writings on religion, I trust that those already familiar with his work will not find the likeness unrecognizable, and that potential readers are unlikely to be deterred by it. More generally, my assessment of Arnold may seem a generous one, even culpably indulgent by some standards. This is partly because in a book of this type there is something to be said for trying to bring out what is interesting, attractive, and valuable in the author concerned, but also because there has in recent years, for reasons I touch on in Chapter 7, been no shortage of hostile or unsympathetic judgements of his work. Since 'supplying what the age most lacks' was one of the animating purposes of Arnold's own critical writings, it seems only right that he in his turn should be the beneficiary of a similar concern.

I should explain, finally, that rather than providing a comprehensive summary of Arnold's 'views', I have throughout concentrated on characterizing the tone and temper of his mind and the distinctive style in which it expressed itself. As I suggest in the first chapter, it is on account of the qualities embodied in his elusive but recognizable literary 'voice', rather than of any body of 'doctrine', that he continues to be such rewarding company for us. Accordingly, I have attempted in the first chapter to characterize this 'voice', to identify its preferred register and habitual strategies, and thus to bring out what is so seductive but also sometimes so irritating about the experience of reading Arnold. To this end, I have allowed myself some longer quotations than may be common in a work of this kind, partly in the spirit of Arnold's injunction that 'the great art of criticism is to get oneself out of the way', but partly also as the best way of coping with the truth of Dr Johnson's observation about the impossibility of doing justice to Shakespeare by means of brief passages: 'He that tries to recommend him by select quotations will succeed like the pedant in Hierocles, who, when he offered his house to sale, carried a brick in his pocket as a specimen.' Thereafter, although Chapters 3 to 6 are thematic rather than strictly chronological in conception, the divisions do very roughly correspond to the four main phases of Arnold's writing life, and this has enabled the biographical account in Chapter 2 to be kept to a minimum.

This book is the expression of an unashamedly personal encounter with Arnold, but I am very conscious of my debts to those far more learned than I am in the byways of Arnoldian scholarship. The sources on which I have drawn most freely are cited in the note on further reading, but I should particularly like to record how much I, in common with all students of Arnold, have profited from the erudition and judgement of R. H. Super and Kenneth Allott in their editions of the prose and poetry respectively. In addition, I am extremely grateful for the generous help and advice of Jane Adamson, John Drury, and Sam Goldberg. I have also greatly appreciated the editorial encouragement of Keith Thomas and the helpfulness of Thomas Webster and his colleagues at Oxford University Press. R. H. Super's careful scrutiny of the completed script enabled me to make several last-minute corrections, though that should not be taken to suggest that he would endorse all that remains.

Arnold once confided to his sister: 'You and Clough are, I believe, the two people I in my heart care most to please by what I write.' I count myself more fortunate in the slightly larger number of those I 'care most to please', since it is the attempt to give them pleasure and earn their commendation which provides the chief (sometimes, it seems, the only) incentive for enduring the agonies of writing. Prefaces conventionally end with the author exempting others from the responsibility for any errors, but since the following friends have not only read the entire manuscript with characteristic attentiveness, but have also done more than they know to shape its author, they must each partly be held to blame for whatever infelicities and misjudgements this book contains: John Burrow, Peter Clarke, Geoffrey Hawthorn, Ruth Morse, John Thompson, Donald Winch.

Contents

Abbreviations

The following abbreviations are used for references from Arnold's writings cited in the text:

The Complete Prose Works of Matthew Arnold, edited by R. H. Super, 11 volumes (Ann Arbor: The University of Michigan Press, 1960–77), cited by volume and page number, e.g. (vi. 264).

The Poems of Matthew Arnold, edited by Kenneth Allott, 2nd edition revised by Miriam Allott (London: Longman, 1979), cited by page number alone, e.g. (283).

L   *The Letters of Matthew Arnold 1848–1888*, collected and arranged by George W. E. Russell, 2 volumes (London: Macmillan, 2nd edn., 1901 [1st edn., 1895]).

UL   *Unpublished Letters of Matthew Arnold*, edited by Arnold Whitridge (New Haven, Conn.: Yale University Press, 1923).

C   *The Letters of Matthew Arnold to Arthur Hugh Clough*, edited by Howard Foster Lowry (London: Oxford University Press, 1932).

N   *The Note-Books of Matthew Arnold*, edited by Howard Foster Lowry, Karl Young, and Waldo Hilary Dunn (London: Oxford University Press, 1952).

1 The Arnoldian voice

With most candidates for 'past masterdom', the claim they now have on our attention rests upon their having originated an influential system of thought or created an enduring literary masterpiece or written some other incontestably great, single work. Honesty might compel us to own up to never having read *The Critique of Pure Reason* or the *Divina Commedia* or *The Decline and Fall of the Roman Empire*, but we readily let the existence of those awesome cultural monuments license an interest in reading about Kant or Dante or Gibbon. The case for Matthew Arnold has to be made in other terms. It is true that in addition to several fine lyric poems and elegies, he wrote at least two minor prose classics which are still widely read, *Essays in Criticism* (1865) and *Culture and Anarchy* (1869). But his achievement did not take the form of one or two great works, and even these two books were collections of essays, most of which had already been published in the periodicals of general culture that were in their heyday in mid-Victorian England. Nearly all his work, in fact, was first published in this way: it is occasional, topical, controversial.

In general, such writing tends to wear badly. The smoke clears, the noise dies down, and all we see is a lone actor on an empty stage still declaiming his now pointless lines. But a remarkable amount of Arnold's writing, especially that dating from the 1860s when he was, in my view, in particularly good voice, soars above the circumstances that prompted it, and moves, instructs, and amuses us still. To read Arnold at his best is to find oneself in the company of a mind of such balance and sympathy that we come, without really noticing, to see experience in his terms, and, unusually, to think the better of ourselves for it. Less original than Coleridge, less prophetic than Carlyle, less profound than Newman, less analytical than Mill, less passionate than Ruskin, less disturbing than Morris—Arnold is more persuasive, more perceptive, more attractive, and more readable than any of his peers.

His writing ranges across several areas that have, in the century since his death, set out their stalls as separate specialisms or disciplines. For want of any better single category, we could call him a 'cultural critic', though both terms might need to be freed from inappropriately narrowing connotations. In the more spacious and accommodating language of his day he was a 'man of letters'. He wrote about politics, he wrote about religion, he wrote, above all, about literature; but he did not write as a political theorist, a theologian, or even, in any restricted sense, a literary critic. He engaged, in an exceptionally alert and responsive way, with most of the important developments in the cultural and intellectual life of Victorian England, yet did so as one who constantly had in mind the standards established by the larger European tradition of thought and letters. For somebody who was drawn into, or in some cases provoked, so many of the now-forgotten controversies of the period, he remained a remarkably consistent and effective critic of the parochial, the self-important, and the merely fashionable. It is because he embodied, as well as recommended, the virtues of a certain cast of mind, a certain way of inhabiting one's identity, that we can, even when he is in full polemical flow, still find him compelling.

Arnold is also frequently ranked alongside Browning and Tennyson as one of the three pinnacles of Victorian verse. He left a far smaller corpus of poetry than either of those copious, at times garrulous, poets, and in fact nearly all of his best work was written in one relatively brief period in his mid- and late twenties. Moreover, his poetry encompasses only a limited range. He does not belong with those poets who stun us with the sheer inventiveness of their imaginations, nor is his work marked by lush imagery or verbal exuberance. As he realized very early, he was never likely to know the kind of popular success as a poet that was enjoyed by his leading contemporaries. He is an intellectual poet, even, it might be said with only a little unfairness, an intellectuals' poet. He writes above all of the melancholy that attends reflection, especially reflection on our inevitable loss of comforting certainties and the capacity for doubt-banishing action. But from this unpromising clay he fashioned some exquisitely poignant verses, several of which, such as 'Dover Beach' or 'The Scholar-Gypsy', will always press their claims on anthologists the world over.

Beyond this, Arnold has become an inescapable, if also oddly nebulous, presence in modern intellectual life. Indisputably, he has exercised an immense, perhaps decisive, influence over our whole way of talking about 'culture' and its role as a possible antidote or corrective to the cramping hold of the narrowly practical and mundane. He, more than any other single writer (including T. S. Eliot, his nearest rival in this respect), endowed the role of the critic with the cultural centrality it now enjoys, particularly in Britain and the United States. The study and teaching, at all levels, of a certain conception and canon of English literature has claimed descent from him, albeit in ways he might not have recognized and would surely not altogether have welcomed. And Arnold's ideas have been invoked in justification of so many of those institutions which have contributed a distinctive, and often distinctively high, tone to the cultural life of modern Britain, such as the BBC, the British Council, and university departments of English. More generally still, the assumptions that have helped to sustain that whole business of the cultivation and diffusion of the literature and cultural legacy of England, which has been such a marked feature of twentieth-century world history, owe much to the inspiration derived from Arnold's writings and example. In recent decades these assumptions have come under fierce attack from several quarters, and Arnold, or a convenient parody of what he is supposed to have stood for, has been the target of some unusually violent criticism. But such abuse has only served to underline how much he, or someone quite like him, has now become an unavoidable cultural reference-point.

In considering the nature of Arnold's claim on our attention, it is important to reiterate that he was not the creator of a theoretical system or body of abstract doctrines (this is one of the reasons he is so badly served by paraphrase). He had too lively an awareness of the pitfalls of systematic abstraction to be pulled very strongly in that direction. 'If all wisdom were come at by hard reasoning' logic would have no rival. But how much

of the blundering to be found in the world comes from people fancying that some idea is a definite and ascertained thing, like the idea of a triangle, when it is not; and proceeding to deduce properties from it, and to do battle about them, when their first start was a mistake! And how

3

liable are people with a talent for hard, abstruse reasoning to be tempted to this mistake! And what can clear up such a mistake except a wide and familiar acquaintance with the human spirit and its productions, showing how ideas and terms arose, and what is their character? and this is letters and history, not logic. (vi. 168)

What, in the end, we must fall back on, he suggested in the various passages in which he urged this point, is 'the judgment which forms itself insensibly in a fair mind along with fresh knowledge'. This quality of 'judgement' is one of the things we value Arnold for, but by its nature it is a quality that does not easily lend itself to the neatly packaged summary (that, of course, may be not the least of its value). Instead, we need to spend some time in his company and to become familiar with his distinctive literary voice. The remainder of this chapter is intended to provide a few suggestions on what to listen for.

We may stay for a moment with this matter of Arnold's lack of a 'system', because, when put as a reproach, it elicited from him some interesting self-descriptions, often expressed in the light, bantering tone which itself carried the main weight of his reply. Here he is in 1865 having his sport with this complaint:

I am very sensible that [my] way of thinking leaves me under great disadvantages in addressing a public composed from a people 'the most logical', says the *Saturday Review*, 'in the whole world'. But the truth is, I have never been able to hit it off happily with the logicians, and it would be mere affectation in me to give myself the airs of doing so. They imagine truth something to be proved, I something to be seen; they something to be manufactured, I as something to be found. I have a profound respect for intuitions, and a very lukewarm respect for the elaborate machine-work of my friends the logicians. I have always thought that all which was worth much in this elaborate machine-work of theirs came from an intuition, to which they gave a grand name of their own. How did they come by this intuition? Ah! if they could tell us that. But no; they set their machine in motion, and build up a fine showy edifice, glittering and unsubstantial like a pyramid of eggs; and then they say: 'Come and look at our pyramid.' And what does one find it? Of all that heap of eggs, the one poor little fresh egg, the original intuition, has got hidden away far out of sight and forgotten. And all the other eggs are addled. (iii. 535)

This is a characteristic passage, not only because what starts out as mock-humble soon turns into high-derisory, but also because it is only likely to persuade those who have already half-felt something similar. Still, even those who find it treads too sharply on their convictions thereby register its weight, though the passage may also suggest that if we are to spend any time in Arnold's company, and enjoy it, we must not be too intolerant of irony and occasional facetiousness.

To attempt to focus on 'doctrine' would, in Arnold's case, also be to go astray in another way. One of the reasons why Arnold can still speak to us more directly than most of his contemporaries is that he did not make the prime object of attention the content of a writer's beliefs so much as the spirit in which they were held. 'What the English public cannot understand is that a man is a just and fruitful object of contemplation much more by virtue of what spirit he is of than by virtue of what system of doctrine he elaborates' (L i. 208). Written shortly after his fortieth birthday, when Arnold was in his pomp, this sentence takes us to the heart of the kind of cultural criticism he was attempting. The reference to 'the English public' calls up his highly-developed sense of audience, while addressing what they 'cannot understand' points towards the animating purpose of his writing life. And then 'a fruitful object of contemplation' is such a characteristic Arnoldian phrase, suggesting an appreciative, open-ended, pondering response, rather than conscripting or subordinating what we read to a partisan programme or single use. With the phrase 'what spirit he is of' we meet, in appropriately informal dress, the core of Arnold's concern: it suggests a cast of mind, but of more than mind—a temper, a way, at once emotional, intellectual, and psychological, of possessing one's experience and conducting one's life. And finally the disparaged 'system of doctrine', something that is, in a telling verb, 'elaborated': it is hard to say whether it is the suggestion of abstraction in 'system' or the hint of the demands of orthodoxy in 'doctrine' that is asking to be swept aside first here.

This sentence, which thus condenses so many of Arnold's concerns, comes from a letter in which he was describing an essay he had just published dealing with the seventeenth-century Dutch philosopher, Spinoza. Spinoza was a Jew; he had a reputation for being an atheist; he had written complex treatises which were thought to encourage immorality. To write about such a figure in

5

a respectable magazine in the religion-drenched England of the mid-nineteenth century was unusual, to write at all favourably was greatly daring. In fact, Arnold was not trying to propagate Spinoza's ideas ('as far as I understand them'), but to indicate the superiority of his generosity of spirit in interpreting the Scriptures, even when allied to what orthodox opinion abhored as his god-lessness, over the narrow but doctrinally impeccable literalism of the approved English exegetes. Spinoza may now seem an odd medium for the message, but in its deliberate attempt to provoke the English public into throwing off its prejudices, especially its religious and political prejudices, sufficiently to benefit from a wider world of ideas, this essay is representative of the task that Arnold set himself as a cultural critic.

There is an important general question here about the degree of distance from one's society required by such a task. A certain reflective detachment is obviously indispensable, but the effective cultural critic needs to be sufficiently intimate with the assumptions and traditions of his society to criticize with the requisite dis-crimination, and he has to share enough of its values to be able to bring them to bear in inducing that kind of self-criticism which is the condition of persuasion. The complete outsider, by contrast, can only denounce; he may disturb those within the walls who hear his curses, but he will not lead them to reform their ways. Arnold was in no sense an outsider: he belonged, by upbringing and style of life, to the most comfortable stratum of the Victorian professional class, mixing easily with the more sympathetic mem-bers of the political and social élite. In intellectual style he was, in Carlyle's adaptation of a Biblical phrase that Arnold was fond of quoting, 'terribly at ease in Zion' (e.g. v. 168). Moreover, he took for granted much that men of his rank and time took for granted. Inevitably, this has left him vulnerable to the reproaches of an age more alert to some of the injustices of class, gender, and race. But it also gave him an insider's ear for significance and nuance, and it meant that he very rarely indulged in that deceptive form of self-flattery which consists in dramatizing oneself as locked in heroically lonely combat with forces that are both alien and overwhelming.

Implicit in Arnold's conception of his task was an ideal of a certain kind of mental and emotional balance. Words like 'partial', 'exclusive', and 'impetuous' recur in his negative characterizations: 'poise' is a favoured positive term. There can be, as we shall see, weakness as well as strength in this. Balance can seem bland and anaemic as an ideal. We may, for example, feel that without a certain kind of one-sided intensity or obsessive pursuit of one idea or one talent, nothing really original or fine is ever done; perhaps, in other words, creativity, originality, and the capacity for intense experience require a *lack* of balance. There are also some intriguing biographical questions about how far such a balance came naturally to Arnold, and how far the 'imperious serenity' which at least one contemporary critic claimed to find in his early poetry was just that. The author of lines like 'Calm is not life's crown, but calm is well' had certainly known tempestuous times, but he also knew their place in a larger scheme. In any event, the mature Arnold took stock of the options in a characteristically even tone:

No-one has a stronger and more abiding sense than I have of the 'daemonic' element—as Goethe called it—which underlies and encompasses our life; but I think, as Goethe thought, that the right thing is, while conscious of this element, and of all that there is inexplicable round one, to keep pushing on one's posts into the darkness and to establish no post that is not perfectly in light and firm. One gains nothing on the darkness by being . . . as incoherent as the darkness itself. (L i. 289)

In translating this general attitude into a charter for criticism, Arnold famously propounded the ideal of 'disinterestedness', that endeavour, as he frequently glossed it, 'to see the object as in itself it really is' (e.g. i. 140). This apparently artless and naïve recipe has come in for more than its share of scorn and even derision in our intellectually suspicious century, but, as so often, our condescension may be misplaced. Arnold did not intend this as an epistemological claim; an empty victory is secured by demonstrating that, according to the latest findings of philosophy and critical theory, objective knowledge is not so easily come by. Arnold's was a more practical, if also more elusive, point about a frame of mind, a state of intention. This frame of mind may in fact be uncommon at any time, for all the lip-service paid to it; certainly Arnold thought it was less than abundant in the intellectual life of Victorian England.

Criticism shows its disinterestedness, as he put it in his famous essay on 'The Function of Criticism at the Present Time' first published in 1864:

by steadily refusing to lend itself to any of those ulterior, political, practical considerations about ideas which plenty of people will be sure to attach to them, which perhaps ought often to be attached to them, which in this country at any rate are certain to be attached to them quite sufficiently, but which criticism has really nothing to do with. (iii. 270)

In responding to the political and intellectual life of his own society, the natural movement of Arnold's mind was away from exaggeration and one-sidedness. 'I hate all over-preponderance of single elements', he exclaimed in a letter of 1865 (L i. 287), declaring an aversion that was at once aesthetic, moral, and intellectual. This meant that there was sometimes a hint of the Higher Counter-Suggestibility about his polemical writing. 'It is delusion . . . which is fatal', and the antidote, the telling of unpopular truths, was always in short supply.

It is not fatal to the Nonconformists to remain with their separated churches; but it is fatal to them to be told by their flatterers, and to believe, that theirs is the one true way of worshipping God, that provincialism and loss of totality have not come to them from following it, or that provincialism and loss of totality are not evils. (v. 254)

There was certainly no danger that Arnold would be cast among the flatterers of the prejudices of his age.

But no less repugnant to him was that partisan habit of mind which he saw constantly at work in the sectarian antagonisms of mid-Victorian England. Nothing is more damaging to the 'free play of the mind on all subjects which it touches' (iii. 270) than the spirit of binary exclusiveness embodied in the tag 'he who is not with us is against us'. Politically, Arnold had broadly Liberal sympathies (a just characterization of his politics is no easy matter, and will be discussed more fully in Chapter 5), but, true to his role and his temperament, he spent far more time undermining the dogmas and curbing the excesses of party-political Liberalism than in showing up the defects of the more obviously unacceptable Tories. His tendency was not at all, as was maliciously said of the nineteenth-century *Times*, 'to be strong on the stronger side'. He was scornful of, for example, those English newspapers which constantly denounced the evils of over-centralized state power, or those French journalists who were always sneering at the weaknesses of autonomous local government: 'It seems to me that they lose their labour, because they are hardening themselves against dangers to which they are neither of them liable' (ii. 17).

By its nature, this urge to correct imbalance will be bound to take different forms in different historical circumstances (as that last example clearly suggests), something that Arnold accepted and worked with in a way that makes him seem surprisingly modern. With some justice, he identified the besetting sins of the public life of Victorian England as parochialism, complacency, and (in a term, borrowed from Heine, which he did much to put into general circulation) philistinism. His response was to try to open up English consciousness to European ideas and perspectives, and to provoke his readers into an uneasy awareness of the limitations of their established mental habits. He did not, therefore, occupy a position that can easily be characterized as 'radical' or 'conservative', in either intellectual or political terms. He was, like most of his educated contemporaries, apprehensive about the possible levelling involved in the as yet untried experiments of democracy and greater social equality, but he had no illusions about the merits of the established order. In any case, it was the inadequacies of the mind that can only think in terms of 'positions' that he pounced upon, and not only the most obvious inadequacies: he knew that radicalism, too, can have its unthinking prejudice and blind loyalty, just as there can be impatience and over-simplification in conservatism. He wrote to enlarge the horizons and expand the sympathies of all 'sides', optimistic that a mind with access to the standards established by 'the best that has been thought and said' could never rest content with partisan simplicities.

In all of this, Arnold's tone of voice was at once his chief weapon and his most distinctive quality. It was not a matter of forcing the reader to abandon one position in favour of another, but of putting him in the way of the experience which, when reflected upon, would bring home to him the defects of the frame of mind that had found expression in the erroneous 'position' in the first place.

It is not that Arnold proposes a series of definitive answers to the great questions of human life, but rather that, by spending time in his company, we begin to be drawn to the habit of mind that emerges from the way in which he handles these questions. When reading his prose, the sense of the engaging conversational presence of the author is exceptionally vivid.

Arnold, as one might expect of such a self-conscious writer, could be knowingly aware of this effect (indeed, a sense of this awareness is sometimes allowed to edge into the prose itself, thereby drawing the reader further into complicity). As his essays began to attract attention, he took the measure of his powers with a frank confidence:

It is very animating to think that one at last has a chance of *getting at* the English public. Such a public as it is, and such a work as one wants to do with it! Partly nature, partly time and study, have also by this time taught me thoroughly the precious truth that everything turns upon one's exercising the power of *persuasion*, of *charm*; that without this all fury, energy, reasoning power, acquirement, are thrown away and only render their owner more miserable. Even in one's ridicule one must preserve a sweetness and good-humour. (L i. 233-4)

Notoriously, the good-humour could seem at best an affectation, at worst a cover. Leslie Stephen turned Arnold's weapon against him when he remarked: 'I often wished . . . that I too had a little sweetness and light that I might be able to say such nasty things of my enemies.' The attempt to charm, in literature as in life, runs a special risk. Argument, when it fails, leaves the reader unconverted; charm, when it fails, leaves him antagonistic, distrustful. More readers have been *irritated* by Arnold than by almost any writer of comparable distinction. G. K. Chesterton registered this exasperation and put his finger near, though not quite on, something crucial when he remarked that 'Arnold kept a smile of heartbroken forbearance, as of a teacher in an idiot-school, that was enormously insulting'. A modern critic, Geoffrey Tillotson, complained representatively that it is Arnold's egotism, clothed in a self-effacing pose, that 'accounts for the high-pitched conversational tone, the ripple of inspired temporisation, the French grace, the lizard slickness'.

What is it about Arnold's writing that has provoked such re-actions? It is something so pervasive, and so much a matter of the chemistry of reader and author, that the reader must read on to see it at work in later chapters, must in fact read Arnold. But one or two extended examples may at least suggest what is at issue. Arnold's playful mockery of his countrymen's philistinism, his criticisms of their educational arrangements, his observations on the significance of England's lack of a body comparable to the *Académie française*, all provoked some understandably snappish responses, as well as some vigorous re-affirmations of the incomparable achievements of the English nation. From a reply first published in 1866, here is Arnold up and going well.

Of course if Philistinism is characteristic of the British nation just now, it must in a special way be characteristic of the representative part of the British nation, the part by which the British nation is what it is, and does all its best things, the middle class. And the newspapers, who have so many more means than I of knowing the truth, and who have that trenchant authoritative style for communicating it which makes so great an impression, say that the British middle class is characterised, not by Philistinism, but by enlightenment; by a passion for penetrating through sophisms, ignoring commonplaces, and giving to conventional illusions their true value. Evidently it is nonsense, as the *Daily News* says, to think that this great middle class which supplies the mind, the will, and the power for all the great and good things that have to be done should want its schools, the nurseries of its admirable intelligence, meddled with. It may easily be imagined that all this, coming on top of the *Saturday Review*'s rebuke of me for indecency, was enough to set me meditating; and after a long and painful self-examination, I saw that I had been making a great mistake. Instead of confining myself to what alone I had any business with,—the slow and obscure work of trying to understand things, to see them as they are,—I had been meddling with practice, proposing this and that, saying how it might be if we established this or that. So I was suffering deservedly in being taunted with hawking about my nostrums of State schools for a class much too wise to want them, and of an Academy for a people who have an inimitable style already. To be sure, I had said that schools ought to be things of local, not State, institution and management, and that we ought not to have an Academy; but that makes no difference. I saw what danger I had been running by thus intruding into a sphere where I have no business, and I resolved to offend in this way no more. (v. 6)

Even at a first reading, we notice several of the qualities that contribute to the distinctive tone here—the light play of irony over the whole passage, the arch references, the self-deprecating mannerisms. What may not at first be so apparent is the way the whole effect depends upon creating a sense of intimacy with the reader, who is drawn to collude in the playfulness. The very fact that some of Arnold's stratagems are so transparent has the effect of flattering us: we are being trusted not to bridle at these flourishes but to appreciate the daring of an author who places himself in our hands in this way. If it works, we are willing to indulge what could otherwise so easily strike us as mere affectation. Sometimes it doesn't work, and with some readers it never works.

Or, to catch him in a quite different mood, here he is in 1878 disposing of some bad writing about Goethe; on the surface, the style could hardly be more direct and baldly classificatory, yet cumulatively it is a passage of great rhetorical forcefulness.

Many and diverse must be the judgments passed on every great poet, upon every considerable writer. There is the judgment of enthusiasm and admiration, which proceeds from ardent youth, easily fired, eager to find a hero and to worship him. There is the judgment of gratitude and sympathy, which proceeds from those who find in an author what helps them, what they want, and who rate him at a very high value accordingly. There is the judgment of ignorance, the judgment of incompatibility, the judgment of envy and jealousy. Finally, there is the systematic judgment, and this judgment is the most worthless of all. The sharp scrutiny of envy and jealousy may bring real faults to light. The judgments of incompatibility and ignorance are instructive, whether they reveal necessary clefts of separation between the experiences of different sorts of people, or reveal simply the narrowness and bounded view of those who judge. But the systematic judgment is altogether unprofitable. Its author has not really his eye upon the professed object of criticism at all, but upon something else which he wants to prove by means of that object. He neither really tells us, therefore, anything about the object, nor anything about his own ignorance of the object. He never fairly looks at it, he is looking at something else. Perhaps if he looked at it straight and full, looked at it simply, he might be able to pass a good judgment on it. As it is, all he tells us is that he is no genuine critic, but a man with a system, an advocate. (viii. 254)

Here, self-assurance rather than playfulness is the dangerous element that may misfire. The almost Augustan cadences of this passage, with its self-consciously balanced syntax and lapidary juxtaposition of declarative clauses, give an air of judicial finality. But if we are prone to feel that our own views are implicitly being slighted by such conclusiveness, and especially if we were already out of sympathy with the point of substance, then the tone merely arouses impatience and resentment.

These passages represent two extremes of Arnold's writing, the same voice speaking in very different tones for different occasions. In between, he was master of a range of effects which were not so purely instrumental as to deserve to be called devices, but which were expressions of his literary personality that can, when confronted with an unsympathetic reader, prove to be two-edged. In replying to the complaint of another contemporary critic, Henry Sidgwick, that sweetness and light were not the world's great need, Arnold could allow a sequence of rhetorical questions to carry his argument for him:

When Mr Sidgwick says so broadly that the world wants fire and strength even more than sweetness and light, is he not carried away by a turn for broad generalisation? does he not forget that the world is not all of one piece, and every piece with the same needs at the same time? It may be true that the Roman world at the beginning of our era, or Leo the Tenth's court at the time of the Reformation, or French society in the eighteenth century, needed fire and strength even more than sweetness and light. But can it be said that the Barbarians who overran the empire needed fire and strength even more than sweetness and light; or that the Puritans needed them more; or that Mr Murphy, the Birmingham lecturer, and his friends, need them more? (v. 180)

The bathos of putting 'Mr Murphy, the Birmingham lecturer' at the climax of this passage is playing for high stakes stylistically, and it is not surprising if some readers have thought that Arnold cheapens his points by being too self-indulgent in his use of such effects.

Nor was he above exploiting the comic potential of inflated titles and funny names. Here he is giving a somewhat rough handling to a sympathetic account of the Mormons.

If he was summing up an account of the doctrine of Plato, or of St Paul, and of its followers, Mr Hepworth Dixon could not be more reverential. But the question is, Have personages like Judge Edmonds, and Newman

Weekes, and Elderess Polly, and Elderess Antoinette, and the rest of Mr Dixon's heroes and heroines, anything of the weight and significance for the best reason and spirit of man that Plato and St Paul have? (v. 149)

By the time we get as far as 'Elderess Polly and Elderess Antoinette' the game is clearly up; the mere juxtaposition of such names with those of Plato and St Paul is a crushing reminder of a lack of perspective in Hepworth Dixon. But it is also, of course, unfair, and the danger is that Arnold's too evident delight in the kill will turn the reader against him. As ever, there can, on Arnold's part, be an element of simple intellectual snobbery in all this; indeed, sometimes, it has to be said, of snobbery *pur*.

Just as Arnold has a variety of ways of projecting an attractive and persuasive sense of himself and his view of the world, so he has an arsenal of ploys for discrediting his opponents without directly engaging in point-by-point refutation of their claims. Often the mere quotation of a victim's view will be sufficient: since it is the defects of a temper or cast of mind he wishes to expose, the simple exhibition of it, especially given the contrast with the more nuanced sensibility implied in Arnold's surrounding prose, will be lethal; and by mercilessly repeating the least happy phrases over and over again, he drowns his opponent in a sea of comic associations.

Another tactic much favoured by Arnold is that of removing a question to higher ground, thereby undercutting his antagonist. For example, to discredit the assertive brass-tacks politics of Liberal MP J. A. Roebuck, he first cites a few particularly unrestrained sentences. ' "I look around me and ask what is the state of England? Is not property safe? Is not every man able to say what he likes? . . . I ask you whether, the world over or in past history, there is anything like it? Nothing. I pray that our unrivalled happiness may last." ' This was taken from that sort of after-dinner political speech in which some pretty complacent things get themselves said, but, not content with exposing it to the chilly reception of print, Arnold immediately moves to higher ground. 'Now obviously there is peril for poor human nature in words and thoughts of such exuberant self-satisfaction'; he then quotes Goethe, company which leaves Roebuck looking grotesque, and concludes, with studied mildness, 'Clearly this is a better line of reflection for weak humanity . . .'. The collusive 'obviously' and 'clearly', the ironic

understatement, the whole holding of Roebuck's vulgar sentiments out at arm's length, all this is devastating. But to that reader for whom the delicately balanced tone has tipped over into a kind of showy sniffiness, it can also seem needlessly irritating.

One cannot read very far into Arnold's prose, however, without recognizing that much the most important, if also potentially the most troublesome, feature of his style is his irony, and this is closely related to his strategy of taking the higher ground mentioned a moment ago. Irony is a particularly vital resource for a writer who wishes to embody as well as recommend an alternative to stridency, exaggeration, and over-simplification. Skilfully used, irony can conjure up the suggestion of much wisdom and judgement held in reserve, accumulated stocks of experience which are not drawn on directly, but which enable the too-simple or too-loud to be seen for what they are. Such a tone came naturally to Arnold, though he was also fully aware of its effectiveness. 'For my part', he reflected in 1867,

I see more and more what an effective weapon, in a confused, loud-talking, clap-trappy country like this, where every writer and speaker to the public tends to say rather more than he means, is *irony*, or according to the strict meaning of the original Greek word, the saying rather less than one means. The main effect I have had on the mass of noisy claptrap and inert prejudice which chokes us has been, I can see, by the use of this weapon. (v. 414)

Sometimes, Arnold's irony is broad almost to the point of burlesque:

I was lucky enough to be present when Mr Chambers brought forward in the House of Commons his bill for enabling a man to marry his deceased wife's sister. . . . His first point was that God's law—the name he always gave to the Book of Leviticus—did not really forbid a man to marry his deceased wife's sister. God's law not forbidding it, the Liberal maxim, that a man's prime right and happiness is to do as he likes, ought at once to come into force, and to annul any such check upon the assertion of personal liberty as the prohibition to marry one's deceased wife's sister. (v. 205)

'Lucky' starts the proceedings with a wink, and thereafter it is downhill all the way for the unfortunate Mr Chambers who spoke so windily of 'God's law'. At other times, the movement of the

eyebrow may at first seem barely perceptible: in commenting on
the tendency of those of narrow culture to devote themselves exclusively to reading the Bible, Arnold could have written that they
'find a great deal in it'; but instead, with a tiny inflection of the
tone, he wrote that they 'make all manner of great discoveries
there' (v. 206). We are left in no doubt about the real magnitude
and worth of these 'discoveries'.

The risk that Arnold runs, of course, is of seeming lofty and
sneering, and once that happens, his 'high-hat persiflage', as it has
been nicely termed, only compounds the offence. Inevitably, those
who are portrayed as being so enamoured of the one great message
they have to tell that they compulsively thrust it at us, like a dog
with a retrieved stick, will resent being patronized. Irony is a
low-temperature medium, and Arnold did not always manage to
prevent its having a slightly chilling effect on our sympathies. But
at its best, his use of irony constantly suggests what it is like to view
a question when we are in reflective possession of great fullness of
experience. We are invited to take a step up and to look back
at an argument that had seemed so compelling when we were
unreflectively meeting it at its own level. In a limited sense, he
seems to say, the argument is no doubt true (the 'limited' and 'no
doubt' signalling that it is a concession that matters little), but
surely we—that collusive, complicitous 'we'—have to recognize
that such truths, inherently one-sided and over-blown as they tend
to be, can be purchased at too high a price.

Arnold's light touch has misled some readers into thinking him
merely flippant. But his 'vivacities' were not only a necessary form
of artistic self-assertion on his part: they were in themselves also an
essential element in the realization of a purpose which was, at
bottom, profoundly serious. He was right to take satisfaction from
the thought that 'however much I may be attacked, my manner
of writing is certainly one that takes hold of people and proves
effective' (L ii. 5). This is the sort of success of which there can be
no objective measurement; indeed, an awareness that the assumptions behind this notion of 'objective measurement' may be
quite inappropriate in this sphere is one of the things Arnold is
particularly good at helping us to understand. Instead, we may
turn to the testimony of a writer who felt sufficient kinship with

Arnold but at the same time distance from him, and who was also graced with the necessary delicacy of spirit, to be capable of discerning and rendering his elusive achievement. What Henry James wrote in 1884 has certainly not become less true in the course of the subsequent century:

All criticism is better, lighter, more sympathetic, more informed in consequence of certain things he has said. He has perceived and felt so many shy, disinterested truths that belonged to the office, to the limited speciality, of no one else; he has made them his care, made them his province and responsibility. . . . When there is a question of his efficacy, his influence, it seems to me enough to ask oneself what we should have done without him, to think how much we should have missed him, and how he has salted and seasoned our public conversation. In his absence the whole tone of discussion would have seemed more stupid, more literal. Without his irony to play over its surface, to clip it here and there of its occasional fustiness, the life of our Anglo-Saxon race would present a much greater appearance of insensibility.

2 The life

'I am still far oftener an object of interest as his son than on my own account' (L i. 161). Matthew Arnold may have been exaggerating a little here in order to give pleasure to his mother, to whom he was writing; but the testimony is none the less striking when we remember that the figure now thought of as the leading Victorian man of letters was already 38 when writing this letter, and that his father had been dead for almost twenty years. Carrying the burden of a famous name can warp and cripple, and Arnold's father did not make things easier for his children by dying at the early age of 47, with his powers and reputation still expanding. But in the course of his own lifetime, Arnold *fils* eventually eclipsed even his father's reputation, and posterity has registered a great disparity in stature between them: Matthew Arnold's writings are now studied and enjoyed from China to Peru, whereas his father is remembered, if at all, as the moulder of a style of school whose modern reputation is equivocal, and as the subject of one of Lytton Strachey's feline portraits in *Eminent Victorians*.

When Thomas Arnold, the world's most famous headmaster, died in 1842, his public standing rested on three main achievements. He was one of the leaders of the 'Broad Church' party in England, opposed to the extremism of Tractarians and Evangelicals alike, advocating inclusion of all groups in a national church that was to provide a cultural and political as well as religious centre for English life. In this role, he had engaged in memorable controversies with John Henry Newman, the most brilliant of the Tractarian theologians; Arnold was a combative man, and England in the 1830s enjoyed a sporting match. Secondly, he was an historian of sufficient note to have been appointed Regius Professor of Modern History at Oxford in 1841. The embodiment of Roman vigour and virtue himself, he published a celebrated *History of Rome* which showed that, as a member of the so-called 'liberal Anglican' school of historians, he had profited from the advanced learning of German scholars like Niebuhr, and owed something to the cyclical theories of Vico. But above all, Thomas Arnold was known as the headmaster of Rugby School, a post to which he had been appointed at the age of 32. He transformed what had been a fair specimen of the debauched and riotous establishments known as public schools into the character-building, God-fearing, scholarship-winning model for the reform in the 1840s and 1850s of other schools of its type. He thereby had an incalculable influence on world history, indirectly staffing an empire, and helping to shape, perhaps to stifle, the emotional development of a governing class for several generations.

Matthew Arnold, second child and eldest son of Thomas and Mary Penrose Arnold, was born on 24 December 1822, at Laleham in the valley of the Thames. An idle and fanciful boy, he survived the experience of being a pupil at his father's school without ever really conforming to its ethos, and in 1841 won a Scholarship to Balliol College, Oxford. Here he could indulge his youthful affectations and dandyish tastes: he rose late, drank much, and read little (or so he wished it to seem). In his final year his friends tried to coach him for his exams, but without making much of a dent in his habits: 'Matt has gone out fishing when he ought properly to be working' (C 29). He got a second-class degree. Some said it was fortunate that his father had not lived to see this, but Arnold characteristically recovered by winning a Fellowship at Oriel in 1845, the college where both his father and Newman had been Fellows, and where his great friend, the poet Arthur Hugh Clough, was currently in residence. But such Fellowships were in those days prizes, not the first steps in a scholarly career, and Arnold continued on his debonair way. Already a keen Francophile, he naturally took himself to Paris, largely, it seems, to follow the career of the famous French *tragédienne*, Rachel, all of whose performances of the French classics in the winter of 1846–7 he attended. Clough, a more troubled soul, shook his head:

Matt is full of Parisianism; theatres in general and Rachel in special: he enters the room with a chanson of Béranger's on his lips—for the sake of French words almost conscious of tune; his carriage shows him in fancy parading the Rue de Rivoli; and his hair is guiltless of English scissors: he breakfasts at 12, and never dines in Hall, and in the week, or 8 days rather (for 2 Sundays must be included), he has been to chapel *once*. (C 25)

As this last phrase suggests, Arnold no longer even outwardly conformed to the piety of his family. He is unusual among early and mid-Victorians in seeming to have slid out of belief in orthodox Christianity at an early age without experiencing any great emotional turmoil. As we shall see (in Chapter 6), he could be deeply responsive to certain kinds of religious emotion, and became increasingly concerned to rescue what was valuable in Christianity generally and in the cultural inheritance of Anglicanism specifically. But his mind seems never to have been scarred by supernatural theology or Biblical literalism.

In 1847, Arnold became personal secretary to a leading Whig politician, Lord Lansdowne, an undemanding post which brought him into the world of high society and allowed him ample time to cultivate the gifts he was discovering in himself as a poet. In 1849 he brought out his first slim volume, *The Strayed Reveller and Other Poems*; it was published anonymously, for fear, it was said, of bringing his father's name into disrepute. In fact, his family were surprised at the evidence of seriousness, yearning, and grief the poems displayed. His poems, of which there were further volumes in 1852 and 1853, spoke of unhappy searchings for a calm place within himself, for the years 1847 to 1851 were Arnold's *Sturm und Drang* period, vividly recorded in his moody, playful, confessional letters to Clough. Falling in love is notoriously a source of both pain and poetry, and Arnold fell in love twice in these years. The 'Marguerite' of his love poems would appear to be art's tribute to the object of the first of these passions: he writes intriguingly to Clough from Switzerland in 1848 that he intends to 'linger one day at the Hotel Bellevue for the sake of the blue eyes of one of its inmates' (C 91). She may have been a young French woman; the fragmentary evidence has teased and titillated biographers ever since. Then, in 1850, he met Frances Lucy Wightman, daughter of a prominent judge; after enduring some of the common delays, indirectness, and obstacles of a Victorian courtship, they were married in 1851. It seems to have been a relatively successful marriage: the chief sorrow of their lives was the death of two sons in 1868, and then of a third, Arnold's favourite, in 1872, a sequence of blows which darkened the spirits of both of them permanently. A son and two daughters survived, and Arnold, an exceptionally affectionate and expressive father, doted on them.

In order to marry, Arnold needed a secure job with an adequate salary. Helped by the patronage of Lord Lansdowne, he was appointed an Inspector of Schools in 1851, thus beginning thirty-five years of what he frequently complained of as 'drudgery', though at other times he acknowledged the benefits of regular work. In the middle of the nineteenth century there were, strictly speaking, no state schools at any level. The limit of public involvement with education was a small annual grant made to various elementary schools, usually denominational in origin and character, which conformed to certain minimal standards. A small group of well-educated gentlemen, often with scholarly or literary inclinations which they continued to pursue, were employed to inspect and report on these schools. Initially, Arnold was responsible for inspecting Nonconformist schools across a broad swathe of central England. He spent many dreary hours during the 1850s in railway waiting-rooms and small-town hotels, and longer hours still in listening to children reciting their lessons and parents reciting their grievances. But this also meant that he, among the first generation of the railway age, travelled across more of England than any man of letters had ever done. Although his duties were later confined to a smaller area, Arnold knew the society of provincial England better than most of the metropolitan authors and politicians of the day.

But drudgery it certainly was. 'I am now at the work I dislike most in the world', he writes to his mother in 1863, 'looking over and marking examination papers. I was stopped last week by my eyes, and the last year or two these sixty papers a day of close handwriting to read have, I am sorry to say, much tried my eyes' (L i. 207). However, the hours and conditions of work were those of the gentlemanly nineteenth-century public service which allowed some time for other pursuits (Peacock and Mill both wrote during office hours at India House, as did Trollope at the Post Office): in the 1860s Arnold would often inspect his schools in the morning and mark his exercises at night, but spend the afternoon at the Athenaeum writing an article. The monotony was interrupted by several extended tours of the Continent to report on educational arrangments there: a five-month visit to France in 1859 was particularly formative for his later social criticism, as well as enabling him to meet Sainte-Beuve, the living critic he most admired. His inspecting duties were also no barrier to his being elected Professor of Poetry at Oxford in 1857, and in the ten years during which he held this largely honorary chair he gave as lectures some of his most enduring essays in literary and social criticism, often sitting up half the night to finish them in time, having already postponed the announced date of a lecture more than once.

In some ways this pattern may have suited Arnold as an author. He could never be one of those writers who chisel and polish a block of prose for years in order to create a few exquisite miniatures in the course of a lifetime. He needed the stimulus of events and controversy. He wrote a good deal—indeed, a remarkable amount for one who was only a part-time writer—and he wrote to cajole, to convince, to controvert, and to pay his bills. While the young poet had sung of the private griefs and yearnings of the solitary, the mature prose-writer moved in a public world whose reference points were the latest number of a periodical, a recent speech in parliament, the season's new books. Nearly all of what we know as Arnold's *books* first appeared in the form of articles in the great monthly journals of general culture, that unrivalled stage upon which so many of the intellectual and literary dramas of mid-Victorian life were acted out. This can, as I have already suggested, sometimes have the result of making his writings a little too full of topical references for the ease of the uninstructed modern reader, but it also means that, since he wrote to be read and not just to be cited in other men's footnotes, his prose is usually lively, often amusing, always accessible.

In the course of the 1860s he acquired a reputation as a critic; by the 1870s he had become a public figure. Of his major works, *Essays in Criticism* had appeared in book form in 1865, *Culture and Anarchy* in 1869, and *Literature and Dogma* in 1873 (these three works will be discussed in Chapters 4, 5, and 6 respectively). He had continued to write poetry in the 1850s, with, as it has seemed to most later readers, steadily lessening inspiration. The stream became a trickle in the 1860s, and then dried up almost entirely.

Commentators ever since have speculated about whether Arnold or the Muse was at fault in their divorce (perhaps Yeats's epigram is relevant: 'We make out of the quarrel with others, rhetoric, but of the quarrel with ourselves, poetry. '). Even in his twenties Arnold had been anxious that age increasingly withered the emotions: when he was 30 he described himself to Clough as 'three parts iced over' (C 128). His later poems, and still more his letters, reveal someone all too aware of the fortitude needed for the long trek across the slope of middle age. The deaths of his children and his turn to religious subjects added their own darker hues. His prose of the later 1870s and 1880s, though it contains some memorably powerful writing, mostly lacked the deftness and light play of irony, including self-irony, that made his earlier work so winning.

His increased fame brought its usual baggage of invitations, honours, and obligations. Fortunately, his taste and talent for sociability never deserted him. As part of his campaign against the assumptions behind English puritanism, Arnold had remarked at one point that 'the wealth of the human spirit is shown in its enjoyments', and his own tastes did not lean towards austerity. He was tall, accounted good-looking, with a charm that owed as much to listening as talking. Even after he had outgrown his dandy phase, he still inclined to high dressing and ran a good deal to fancy waistcoats. He was very responsive to the charms of beautiful women (albeit in his later writings increasingly censorious of sexual misconduct, especially among the 'lubricious' French), and he particularly liked champagne. While in America in 1883, he was reported to have scandalized the elders of the 'dry' college town where he was staying when he was asked what he would like after his lecture and replied 'Whisky'. In characterizing him, some found that the word 'fop' came to mind very easily, and some took his wit as a sign of a lack of seriousness, as some always will. Charlotte Brontë had been more perceptive in finding 'a real modesty beneath the assumed conceit'. Those who knew him well concurred in emphasizing his warmth and gaiety, as well as a sentimentality which, while it could be a blemish in the poet, was lovable in the man.

By the 1880s he was recognized as England's premier man of letters. He capitalized on this with a lecture-tour in America, which earned him a substantial sum (of which he was always more or less urgently in need), but few fresh admirers: he was not a good lecturer, and Americans found him mannered. It did not help his popularity that his assessment of American civilization had always been frankly unflattering. In England he was offered, and after much hesitation accepted, a small civil list pension 'in public recognition of service to the poetry and literature of England'. In 1886 he was, to his great relief, finally able to retire from school-inspecting; although two of his reports on foreign schools had proved to be of such weight as to warrant republication in book form, his official career had been undistinguished, with promotions coming late and seldom. He had long had to contend with warnings from the hereditary heart condition which had carried off both his father and grandfather, and it finally killed him in Liverpool on 15 April 1888. He was buried at Laleham, alongside his three children; a special train brought an impressive body of mourners from London, including Robert Browning and Henry James. Memorial tributes were more than conventionally generous, the most apposite, perhaps, being that of Benjamin Jowett, the Master of Balliol College, Oxford, who was not known for his fulsomeness: 'No-one ever united so much kindness and light-heartedness with so much strength. He was the most sensible man of genius I have ever known.'

3 The poet

The collected prose works of Matthew Arnold occupy eleven fat volumes; the complete poetry, even when fleshed out with notes, variants, and appendices, fits easily into one volume in any of the several modern editions in which it has appeared. Though any rounded account of his achievement must to some extent reflect these proportions, such crude quantities tell us little about the relative value or enduring appeal of his various compositions in the two genres. In fact, the reputation of his poetry has been more stable and more generally favourable over the past hundred years than that of his prose, even though, as I have suggested, I think it is now the latter which has the greater claim on our attention. But certainly there may still be some readers who, vaguely recalling 'Dover Beach' or 'The Scholar-Gypsy' from school anthologies, are surprised to find he 'also' wrote prose.

Arnold's poetry, as we have seen, belongs very largely to the earliest stage of his adult life; most of his best pieces are contained in the three slim volumes he published in 1849, 1852, and 1853, all written before his thirtieth birthday. It is true that in the mid- and late 1850s Arnold wrote some of his longest dramatic and narrative poems, but these have never found much favour. In 1867 he published a volume entitled *New Poems*, which contained several fine individual pieces, but even some of these (including 'Dover Beach' and 'Stanzas from the Grande Chartreuse') had almost certainly been largely written before 1853. Much of his poetry recounts an inner struggle to find some equilibrium, but its conclusion, both discursively and in practice, was that balance was only to be found, or only came upon him (since it was not so entirely a matter of will as the poems at times suggest), when he committed himself to the world, to action, to mundane existence—to, in short, prose, with all the overtones that word can carry of the ordinary, the practical, the flat. Part of the poignancy of Arnold's biography comes from the fact that he never ceased to have the sensibilities and yearnings of a poet, though he largely ceased to write poetry. He lived the greater part of his life knowing that 'the Muse be gone away' (578).

Despite both the limited quantity and, in a sense to be explained in a moment, the restricted range of Arnold's poetry, he has always been regarded as one of the major poets of the nineteenth century, and has indeed usually been accorded a secure place in the second rank of English poetry, no inconsiderable achievement for one who devoted the greater part of his creative energies to other genres. In the best of his lyrics and elegies the experience of reflective sadness is rendered with touching melodic aptness, while even those poems which are uneven wholes sometimes contain lines that make us want to read on and to know more about a poet of such intriguingly erratic gifts.

Moreover, Arnold's poetry continues to have scholarly attention lavished upon it, in part because it seems to furnish such striking evidence for several central aspects of the intellectual history of the nineteenth century, especially the corrosion of 'Faith' by 'Doubt'. No poet, presumably, would wish to be summoned by later ages *merely* as an historical witness, but the sheer intellectual grasp of Arnold's verse renders it peculiarly liable to this treatment. In an exceptionally frank, but not unjust, self-assessment in a letter to his mother in 1869, Arnold himself almost predicted this historical role for his poetry:

My poems represent, on the whole, the main movement of mind of the last quarter century, and thus they will probably have their day as people become conscious to themselves of what that movement of mind is, and interested in the literary productions which reflect it. It might be fairly urged that I have less poetical sentiment than Tennyson, and less intellectual vigour and abundance than Browning; yet, because I have perhaps more of a fusion of the two than either of them, and have more regularly applied that fusion to the main line of modern development, I am likely enough to have my turn, as they have had theirs. (L ii. 9)

Those who find Arnold's poetry unsympathetic might be inclined to respond that its chief defect lies precisely in the way it arises too exclusively from a movement of *mind*.

'*The dialogue of the mind with itself*'

Although he wrote in several poetic genres—sonnets, lyrics, elegies, extended narrative poems, verse drama and so on—Arnold's range as a poet was limited in two ways: he largely dealt with a confined set of themes, and to a great extent he wrote in one readily recognizable register or voice. Before considering certain particular aspects of his poetic achievement, it may be well to try to characterize the nature of these themes and this voice in very general terms.

The dominant note of Arnold's best poetry is reflection on loss, frustration, sadness. It is important from the start to draw attention to 'reflection', because his poems nearly always are, even if not explicitly, second-order reflections on the nature or meaning of certain kinds of experience, rather than expressions or records of that experience itself. When Arnold spoke, famously, of modern poetry as 'the dialogue of the mind with itself' (i. 1), he coined a phrase that irresistibly asks to be applied to his own writing. At the same time, and in a spirit with which later generations have become more rather than less familiar, the poetry frequently expresses a desperate, eternally self-defeating desire to escape from this unending round of intellection, from being 'prisoners of our consciousness' (200).

A recurrent symbolic landscape operates both as a backdrop and a load-bearing metaphorical structure in Arnold's chief lyrics and elegies, a landscape which, when reduced to its bare elements, maps the three stages of life's journey. That journey is characteristically represented by a river, which rises in a cool, dark glade, flows out on to the fierce, hot plain, and then finds its way to the wide, calm sea. These are three periods of the individual's life, but also three stages in historical growth more generally: as described in the standard modern commentary on the three phases of this symbolism, 'the first is a period of joyous innocence when one lives in harmony with nature, the second a period of suffering when one is alone in a hostile world, and the third a period of peace in which suffering subsides into calm and then grows up into a new joy, the joy of active service in the world'.

But Arnold's poetry also returns to certain favoured settings which are symptomatic rather than symbolic in this sense. For example, the implied or explicit location of the persona speaking a particular poem frequently turns out to be on a mountain-top or other lofty place, the natural habitat of reflection and of those searching for the wide comprehending view. 'From some high station he looks down', as he says of 'the poet' in the early 'Resignation' (95), but of course both 'lofty' and 'looking down' also suggest a relation to the world which is not purely a matter of altitude, and Arnold has been accused of viewing suffering humanity a little too much *de haut en bas*. Similarly, his marked taste for the ambience of cool, moonlit settings (a staple of Romantic poetry that becomes almost a cliché with Arnold) reveals as well as represents. In Arnold's symbolic economy, such settings are obviously intended to contrast with or provide an escape from the hot, dusty scenes of bustling workaday life, but their coolness and brightness can easily start to seem chill, the light a little too clinical. We are reminded that in this setting the yearned-for transforming emotion which would enable us to escape ourselves can only be reflected upon, not experienced.

Another way to consider the limits of Arnold's range (tastes vary on whether these should also be regarded as limitations) is to observe how much of his poetic diction depends upon a kind of Romantic thesaurus: much use is made of stage-properties like moons and graves, tears flow a little too freely (no less than 68 times, according to one count), and there is embarrassingly frequent resort to the mannered interjection 'Ah!'. It is also noticeable, especially in some of his less successful pieces, how much of the weight of tone and meaning is carried by the adjectives, often in the form of past participles, rather than by the verbs, where he relies a good deal on the blandest or least energizing forms like 'was', 'had', and (an Arnoldian favourite) 'seemed'. These combine with the past participles to reinforce the elegiac sense of a world in which nothing is now happening: it is already all over before the poem starts, whether through death or loss or—not a trivial feature of Arnold's dominant poetical mood—simple belatedness.

Arnold was a self-conscious poet, arguably a learned poet, and thus inevitably preoccupied with his relation to his great predecessors. 'Predecessors', for the young poet of the 1840s, meant, overwhelmingly, the English Romantics. Needless to say, Arnold's poetic sympathies and, in certain senses, debts were wide: he felt the length of the shadow of the Greeks as much as any Englishman in his Greece-obsessed century; he displayed a responsive affinity to Virgil's gentle pastoral melancholy; he, somewhat exceptionally, was selectively appreciative of Goethe's verse, as well as holding him in something like awe as a cultural hero; and the list could be extended. But the English Romantics, perhaps Byron and Keats even more than Shelley or Coleridge, were his mind's familiar companions and left permanent echoes in his ear. Above all, the inescapable poetic presence for Arnold was Wordsworth. In literary terms, his relationship to Wordsworth bordered on the filial, a connection strengthened by early visits to him from the Arnolds' neighbouring family home in the Lake District, but more significantly intensified by Arnold's implicit association of Wordsworth with the early stage of human innocence, and with the simple, joyful song which that age still allowed. This surfaced most visibly in the 'Memorial Verses' Arnold wrote following Wordsworth's death in 1850, where it is 'The freshness of the early world' which Wordsworth, the poet of childhood recollected in maturity, is credited with restoring to us.

> He laid us as we lay at birth
> On the cool flowery lap of earth. . . .

But the power to re-create the immediacy of this primitive experience is one which Arnold's 'time-ridden consciousness' now regards as irrecoverably lost. Possibly others may arise to do for later generations what Byron and Goethe did for theirs,

> But where will Europe's latter hour
> Again find Wordsworth's healing power?
> Others will teach us how to dare,
> And against fear our breast to steel;
> Others will strengthen us to bear —
> But who, ah! who, will make us feel? (242)

The slight awkwardness of the syntax of 'against fear our breast to steel' is characteristic of Arnold's verse, though for once the interjection 'ah!', complete with its over-insistent exclamation-mark, manages not to seem affected here, or introduced merely to accommodate the rhythm.

The relation to Wordsworth has an interpretative as well as biographical significance, and it helps us fix the sense in which Arnold should be regarded as a post-Romantic as well as, more straightforwardly, a late-Romantic poet. For example, although he pays homage to some of the same aspects of nature's 'healing power', and even celebrates some of the same associations of the English countryside, the relation to nature revealed in Arnold's poetry is quite different from that characteristic of Wordsworth's. In Arnold's work, nature figures either as a reinforcing backdrop for the dialogue of the mind with itself, or else as a set of symbols on to which man's travails and hopes are transposed. It is never immediately at one with man, nor is it infused with a deeper life of its own. In fact, Arnold tries to make nature, too, into a good Stoic: the nature that 'seems to bear rather than rejoice' has learned to keep a stiff upper lip. For all its recourse to the standard Romantic scenery, Arnold's poetry is pre-eminently that of emotion re-collected indoors.

Moreover, where memory, in Wordsworth's poetry, can refresh by bringing back the flavours of a more nourishing or soothing moment, thus easing our passage through an uncongenial world, for Arnold memory itself is usually a painful reminder of the utter unrecoverability of experience: far from refreshing, it merely provides another occasion for self-conscious wistfulness. There are, of course, many possible sources of the feeling that, poetically, one has come too late, but it is particularly characteristic of the post-Romantic sensibility in general and Arnold's in particular to blame the curse of reflectiveness for making certain kinds of pure or unmediated satisfaction permanently unattainable.

Of love and loss

The two poetic forms in which Arnold is commonly held to have excelled are the lyric and the elegy. That traditional division is, however, somewhat misleading in Arnold's case: exaggerating to bring out the point, one could say that most of his lyrics are really elegies too. That is, his characteristic preoccupation as a poet is so much with transience and loss that he writes in a recognizably elegiac manner even when not formally writing about the dead. But, more suggestively, there is a sense in which many of his finest lyrics are not really about what they seem to be about. The point can be made most tellingly by considering the set of poems Arnold wrote on that most traditional of themes for the lyric—love.

Those short pieces which Arnold later grouped as a sequence under the heading 'Switzerland' ostensibly record successive stages of the love-affair with 'Marguerite'. They do, certainly, contain many of the conventional tropes of the genre, such as the lover's fond inventory of his loved one's attributes:

> The sweet blue eyes—the soft, ash-coloured hair—
> The cheeks that still their gentle paleness wear—
> The lovely lips with their arch smile that tells
> The unconquered joy in which her spirit dwells . . . ('Parting', 125)

But as we reread these poems, the unsettling thought comes over us that they are not really about Marguerite, nor even about the experience of being in love. They are reflections upon how even this kind of experience—it is part of their unsatisfactoriness as love poems that Arnold didactically classifies it as a *kind* of experience, rather than being overwhelmed by its uniqueness—affords no real escape from the self and its oppressive sense of isolation. Although they effectively exploit the lightness and vigour of crisp mountain air and rushing, snow-fed streams, the Switzerland sequence is ultimately dark in tone, a sombre reflection about the inconsolable spiritual isolation which had hoped to find a cure in love, but which, chastened by failure, has now been thrown back upon a deeper self-examination.

Revealingly, several of the poems in this set are doubly retro-spective: they are not only, in an obvious sense, reflections on a past experience, but it turns out that that experience itself is already one of rumination prompted by some event subsequent to the experience being ruminated upon. Meeting 'Marguerite' a year later is the most obvious of these reflection-provoking events: the 'still' in the above lines marks both the passage of time and a reflective awareness of the shifting relation of memory and reality. This soon develops into a more comprehensive reflection, in which the focus retreats from the outer world of the lovers' situation to the inner world of self-knowledge:

> Far, far from each other
> Our spirits have grown;
> And what heart knows another?
> Ah! who knows his own? (126)

Even in these relatively early poems, we can see that love figures as what has been nicely termed 'a sort of mournful cosmic last resort', but one that is, like all earlier possible refuges, ultimately doomed to prove unsatisfactory.

Where, at their best, the 'Marguerite' poems excel is in conveying the poignancy of these sentiments by certain simple yet haunting rhythms rather than by explicit argument. Despite its somewhat mannered title, 'To Marguerite—Continued' constitutes a particularly happy example of this quality. The first stanza states the Arnoldian preoccupation succinctly:

> Yes! in the sea of life enisled
> With echoing straits between us thrown
> Dotting the shoreless watery wild
> We mortal millions live *alone*. (130)

Among the details that contribute to the effect here, we may particularly remark the randomness suggested by 'dotting', the homeless infinity behind 'shoreless', the unnerving transfer of the 'wild', trackless and inhospitable, from land to sea, and the brilliant near-oxymoron of the 'millions' who live 'alone'.

The subtle effect of the rhythms tells to even greater effect in the last stanza, which concludes with one of the most beautiful lines that Arnold ever wrote:

> Who ordered that their longing's fire
> Should be, as soon as kindled, cooled?
> Who renders vain their deep desire?
> A God, a God their severance ruled!
> And bade betwixt their shores to be
> The unplumbed, salt, estranging sea. (130–1)

The iambic beat of this is at first regular and almost clipped, with a faintly Augustan flavour to the neat antithesis of 'kindled/cooled'. But the minor caesura at mid-line following 'salt' is, in both senses, arresting; the effect at first seems angular, but then registers as a lightly-sustained diminuendo. This, together with the fathomless 'unplumbed', the unwelcoming 'salt', the discordant 'estranging', all call up dimensions of loneliness in a line that has a wonderful sense of inevitability to it.

The second, much shorter and generally less successful, sequence of love poems (entitled, banally, 'Faded Leaves') moves even further away from the experience itself in its meditation on the tantalizing power of recalled emotion. The additionally elegiac note here comes from the anguished sense that even memory is only an imperfect reminder that there was, once, an emotion which briefly impinged on our isolation, but that *no* feeling can be preserved or re-created, not even the feeling of love. The most effective of this set is the simple 'Too Late', where larger reflections on transience and the unarrestability of experience do not choke a more directly expressed pain:

> Each on his own strict line we move,
> And some find death ere they find love;
> So far apart their lives are thrown
> From the twin soul which halves their own.
>
> And sometimes, by still harder fate,
> The lovers meet, but meet too late.
> —Thy heart is mine! — *True, true! ah, true!*
> —Then, love, thy hand! — *Ah no! adieu!* (245)

But the immediacy of this last stanza is rare among Arnold's so-called 'love poems', a further indication that they are not essentially *about* love (a point I shall return to at the end of this chapter). Whatever may have been true of Arnold the man, the poet almost seems to treat his ideal of love as a state of *diminished* rather than of heightened emotion:

> How sweet to feel, on the boon air,
> All our unquiet pulses cease!
> To feel that nothing can impair
> The gentleness, the thirst for peace. (134)

In the same poem, in which the speaker imagines being re-united in another life with the woman for whom he has experienced an unrequited or unsatisfactory love in this life, the deeper sympathy which the lovers might then discover between themselves is referred to as being 'Ennobled by a vast regret'. That 'regret' provides the keynote of these lyrics, and it is revealing of the sensibility that can turn even love-poems into elegies that Arnold should choose to dwell upon its 'ennobling' power.

33

This sensibility found less problematic expression in the best-known of Arnold's actual elegies, such as the pastoral 'The Scholar-Gipsy' (composed in 1852-3) and its companion piece 'Thyrsis' (probably written 1864-5, in commemoration of Clough, who had died in 1861). Extended discussion of these poems is not possible here, but it is worth remarking that they, too, share with the love-poems the quality of having a deeper preoccupation than their ostensible subjects. What unites them, apart from Arnold's explicit commentary and their use of the same unusual Keats-inspired stanza form, is their celebration of the countryside around Oxford and its association with the untrammelled responsiveness of the young poets who roamed the hills together in the early and mid 1840s. But in fact both poems constantly return to meditating upon the unrecoverability of this youthful aestheticism, and around both poems, but especially 'Thyrsis', there hovers the suggestion of sentimental indulgence in nostalgia and regret for its own sake— 'let me give my grief its hour' (543). In a letter to one of their mutual friends, Arnold acknowledged a little defensively that 'one has the feeling, if one reads the poem as a memorial poem, that not enough is said about Clough in it' (L i. 327). As this suggests, the poem is less an elegy for a dead friend, than a lament for a lost youth, the poet's *own* youth. The meditation soon takes on the stylized pathos of youth-recollected-in-maturity, with

> The heart less bounding at emotion new
> And hope, once crushed, less quick to spring again.
>
> And long the way appears, which seemed so short
> To the less practised eye of sanguine youth; (545)

'Thyrsis' was the last of Arnold's really successful major poems, but its theme, and even to some extent its mood, had been evident in his poetry from the start. Arnold may have written his best poetry when young, but, given his sustained preoccupation with transience and loss, there is a sense in which he never was a young poet.

'Empedocles on Etna'

A special place in Arnold's poetic *œuvre* is occupied by his long dramatic poem 'Empedocles on Etna'. This is partly because it is such a brilliant dramatization of Arnold's own internal conflicts (though it would be a mistake, of course, simply to reduce the poem to such biographical elements, or to identify the author too closely with any one of its characters); but it is also because he thrust additional significance on the poem by withdrawing it almost immediately after its first publication in 1852. The austere classicism of the Preface to the 1853 collection was in part a justification of his decision to omit 'Empedocles' from that volume; he treated it as the epitome of that modern dwelling upon one's own hesitations and uncertainties whose fruitlessness could only be remedied by returning to the portrayal of great actions. Thereafter, Arnold did not republish the poem until 1867, when he expressly included a note explaining that it now appeared 'at the request of a man of genius . . . Mr Robert Browning' (156). It is a sign of the intensity of Arnold's eddying struggles over his identity in the early 1850s, which found expression in the perversely self-repudiating 1853 Preface, that he should omit what has since come to be regarded as a major part of his poetic achievement and one of the most significant long poems of the nineteenth century.

Although Arnold subtitled 'Empedocles' 'a dramatic poem', 'dramatic' is something of a misnomer. Despite being divided into two 'acts' and being put into the mouths of three 'characters', there is really no 'action', but rather an uninterrupted series of discursive monologues. (Actually, something similar could be said of many of Arnold's so-called 'narrative poems' too, which are really extended reflections only very loosely hung on a narrative frame.) In effect, 'Empedocles' takes the usual Arnoldian 'dialogue of the mind with itself' and puts the different sides of the discussion into the mouths of different speakers. Empedocles himself, who speaks the greater part of the poem, attempts, despite the contrary promptings of his own creative aspirations, to represent in an attractive light the stoicism necessary to confront the increasing burden of joyless life that comes with maturity. He preaches this message to his disciple, Pausanias, who, as a physician and therefore someone who lives in the world of action, is able to confront the prospect fairly cheerfully, which Empedocles himself is notably unable to do. The third character, a young poet named Callicles, expresses the untroubled joy of the creator living entirely in the realm of the aesthetic, a position

Empedocles moodily regards as incompatible with increasing maturity.

The three scenes are set at successively higher points on the slopes of Mount Etna, until, in the final scene, Empedocles, unable to resolve the conflicting demands of his sensibilities and his reason into a livable life, throws himself into the crater of the volcano. The meaning of Empedocles' suicide for the interpretation of the poem as a whole has continued to divide commentators, some seeing it as an endorsement of Empedocles' analysis of the irreconcilable conflicts within existence, while others take it as a more robust condemnation of his inability to engage with the world as it is. Perhaps a more detached, philosophic, reading of the outcome is suggested by the obviously important fact that the last lines of the poem are given to Callicles, who sings of the continuing, impersonal, existence of the whole of creation, 'What will be for ever; / What was from of old', concluding with the cosmic closure of

> The day in his hotness,
> The strife with the palm;
> The night in her silence,
> The stars in their calm. (206)

Significantly, the last word of this whole troubled poem is thus 'calm', the quality which Arnold at this point so uncalmly sought and failed to find.

Part of the fascination of the poem lies in the way the verse constantly signals that Empedocles cannot give his real emotional assent to the stoic resignation he ostensibly commends. His official creed is essentially that of the ancient Stoic philosopher Epictetus (an author whom Arnold had recently been reading with growing sympathy), laced with a dash of the work-ethic of Carlyle. It offers deliberately low-key satisfactions: man must not 'fly to dreams, but moderate desire', and so

> I say: Fear not! Life still
> Leaves human effort scope.
> But, since life teems with ill,
> Nurse no extravagant hope;
> Because thou must not dream, thou need'st not then despair! (182)

Empedocles himself, however, is cursed with a kind of intellectual nostalgia, a yearning for (and reluctance to accept the disappearance of) more animating creeds, held with livelier conviction. He is still tormented by the memory, and sometimes more than the memory, of the struggle between the 'impetuous heart' and the 'contriving head'. Callicles observes that Empedocles' railing is not adequately accounted for by the state of the world:

> There is some root of suffering in himself,
> Some secret and unfollowed vein of woe,
> Which makes the time look black and sad to him. (163)

One source of Empedocles' 'secret and unfollowed vein of woe' is his sense of his 'dwindling faculty of joy'. Suffocated by the inescapable nightmare of consciousness, he fears he is 'a living man no more',

> Nothing but a devouring flame of thought--
> But a naked, eternally restless mind. (200)

He searches for that sense of 'poise' that was, when characterized a little differently, to be such a crucial value in Arnold's critical writings, but in his most anguished moments Empedocles knows that

> . . . only death
> Can cut his oscillations short, and so
> Bring him to poise. (196)

In one of the fiercest passages in the whole poem, Empedocles bitterly ruminates on how, though the body may die and return to the elements whence it came, mind and thought will live on:

> Where will *they* find their parent element?
> What will receive *them*, who will call *them* home?

And so

> . . . we shall unwillingly return
> Back to this meadow of calamity,
> This uncongenial place, this human life;
> And in our individual human state
> Go through the sad probation all again,
> To see if we will poise our life at last,
> To see if we will now at last be true

37

> To our only true, deep-buried selves,
> Being one with which we are one with the whole world;
> Or whether we will once more fall away
> Into some bondage of the flesh or mind,
> Some slough of sense, or some fantastic maze
> Forged by the imperious lonely thinking power,
> And each succeeding age in which we are born
> Will have no more peril for us than the last; (201-2)

Pausanias, a more robust, active figure, can cheerfully accept the limitations of such a creed and implicitly live by it. Empedocles' own broodings drive him inexorably to a choice between a spirit-numbing, poetry-killing compromise with a drab world — or death, which allows the preservation of at least some kind of integrity of passion. Finally, he works free from the toils of reflection: he knows that he 'breathes free', if only for a moment, and to (as it were) commit himself to that moment 'ere the mists of despondency and gloom' begin to choke him once more, he throws himself into the crater (204).

But Arnold, of course, does not. By this I mean not only the rather obvious point that what Arnold 'does' is to write 'Empedocles on Etna', thus attempting to shape some whole in which these conflicting choices can be realized and held in a satisfying tension; but also that Arnold *did* 'turn to the world'. His acceptance of the all-too-mundane post of school-inspector in order to get married can be seen, in this light, as something of a 'philosophic act'. Auden famously quipped that Arnold the poet 'thrust his gift in prison till it died'. But it may be nearer the mark to suggest that it was precisely during his poetically creative years that Arnold most acutely *felt* trapped in 'the hot prison of effortful life', and that the poetry was a kind of protest against the possibility that mind and thought will forever 'keep us prisoners of our consciousness' (200). The poetry and the unresolved unhappiness went together; it was accepting the prison that ultimately provided some release. Arnold did not throw himself into the crater; rather, he turned to writing prose.

'*Wandering between two worlds*'

After the inner turmoil that accompanied his transition from dandyish young late-Romantic poet to burden-shouldering man of affairs in the early and mid 1850s, Arnold tried various poetic experiments which, it now seems clear, were forced against the grain of his talent. Following the injunction of his 1853 Preface to leave behind the crippling introspection of modern thought, he took his subjects from Norse sagas and Greek history. The first issued in his rather leaden epic 'Balder Dead' (damned for ever by one wag as 'Balder Dash'); the second in his attempt to reproduce the grandeur of ancient tragedy in his verse-drama *Merope*. This last has been universally judged a poetic failure, though an impressive technical achievement: a skilful re-creation of original instruments but a lifeless pastiche of early music. Swinburne long ago set the tone of subsequent response to the piece when he teased, 'The clothes are well enough, but where has the body gone?' *Merope* pays homage to, but only limply embodies, some of the qualities that Arnold most admired in Greek literature (a topic to be discussed more fully in Chapters 4 and 5 below), and it has some of the smooth coolness and clear lines of an alabaster statue; but, as with most things in alabaster, one is constantly aware that one is looking at a reproduction.

Although the 1867 volume *New Poems* is generally thought to include much that fell below the standard of Arnold's earlier volumes, it did contain a few poems that have since become among his best-known pieces, notably 'Dover Beach' (probably written as early as 1851, though the evidence is inconclusive), and the thematically linked but poetically more discursive 'Stanzas from the Grande Chartreuse' (largely composed in 1852). Familiar as these poems may be, they demand discussion here not only on account of their intrinsic merits, but also because they are such representative expressions of some of Arnold's deepest preoccupations.

It is, of course, hard now to see 'Dover Beach' with anything like fresh eyes, so much a part of our familiar poetic stock has it become. The organizing trope of the poem, the way in which the retreat of the tide-driven sea suggests the withdrawing of 'the Sea of Faith', employs a favoured Arnoldian metaphor. A sequence of monosyllables joined by simple verbs establishes the encompassing peacefulness of the setting:

> The sea is calm tonight.
> The tide is full, the moon lies fair
> Upon the straits; on the French coast the light
> Gleams and is gone; the cliffs of England stand,
> Glimmering and vast, out in the tranquil bay. (254)

The very stillness of the scene invites that mood of reflective sadness at which Arnold excelled. Indeed, the 'grating roar' of the shingle on the beach, and the movement of the waves themselves as they 'Begin, and cease, and then again begin', brings 'The eternal note of sadness in'. It leads the speaker to reflect, as the poem gathers intellectual and rhythmic intensity, how 'The Sea of Faith / Was once, too, at the full'; and then, in a haunting evocation of bleak absence, come the famous lines:

> But now I only hear
> Its melancholy, long, withdrawing roar,
> Retreating, to the breath
> Of the night-wind, down the vast edges drear
> And naked shingles of the world. (256)

Ostensibly, love is then invoked as the only solace, but almost immediately this comes to seem something of a perfunctory gesture, as it is swallowed up by the gathering momentum of the poem's powerfully dark picture of our homelessness in a cold, indifferent world.

> . . . for the world, which seems
> To lie before us like a land of dreams,
> So various, so beautiful, so new,
> Hath really neither joy, nor love, nor light,
> Nor certitude, nor peace, nor help for pain;
> And we are here as on a darkling plain
> Swept with confused alarms of struggle and flight,
> Where ignorant armies clash by night. (257)

Interestingly, though the rhythm and cadence of 'Dover Beach' have cast their spell even over some of the unwillingly-conscripted readers of school anthologies, the poem is unusually hard to analyse in formal terms. It is, as the standard edition describes it, 'a lyric consisting of four unequal verse-paragraphs, irregularly rhymed. Lines vary between two and five stresses, but more than half the lines are five-stressed' (254). This dry, technical description cannot take us very far, but since there is no doubt that Arnold's ear could at times let him down very badly, his command of the emotion-sprung rhythm of 'Dover Beach' is all the more striking precisely for *not* being able to take its structure from one of the established verse-forms. Is it significant or merely curious that it should be Arnold, advocate of an austere classicism and polished cultivator of the most traditional genres, who should thus be credited with the first major 'free-verse' poem in the language?

With 'Stanzas from the Grande Chartreuse', it is hard not to feel that Arnold's relation to 'the Age of Faith' is a little more equivocal than it may at first appear. While the poem laments the impossibility of ever again inhabiting an animating faith in the way his imagined monks did, it also condescends a little to the credulity of earlier ages, and thus introduces a slight note of self-congratulation. We may be deprived, but we are not deceived. The monks, 'Last of the people who believe', are no doubt fortunate, but at least those like Arnold, 'Last of the race of them who grieve', can savour the bitter-sweet taste of a yet more exquisite emotion, that special pathos that attaches to being the last of a line. Though the poet famously characterizes himself as

> Wandering between two worlds, one dead,
> The other powerless to be born,' (305)

he surely takes a subtle, if perverse, pleasure in his stranded state, and would not, now, exchange his lot for that of the credulous monk or the indifferent unbeliever. R. H. Hutton, always the most perceptive of Arnold's contemporary critics, was pointing in the same direction when he unfavourably contrasted 'the true humility of the yearning for faith' with Arnold's 'grand air of tearful Virgilian regret'.

For this as well as other reasons, Arnold may be a more doubtful, or perhaps just a more subtle, witness of the intellectual dilemmas of his age than historians have always allowed. But certainly some of the deepest spirits of his own and the immediately succeeding generation, not least among them George Eliot, found that Arnold's poetry spoke to their anxieties and yearnings with a special power. Hutton again forces his way to the front with the rhetorical excess of the natural spokesman:

When I come to ask what Mr Arnold's poetry has done for this generation, the answer must be that no one has expressed more powerfully and poetically its spiritual weaknesses, its craving for a passion it cannot feel, its admiration for a self-mastery it cannot achieve, its desire for a creed that it fails to accept, its sympathy with a faith it will not share, its aspiration for a peace it does not know.

'*Heroic egotism*'

We have already seen that the ostensible subject-matter of many of Arnold's lyrics and elegies proves, on closer examination, not really to be the governing preoccupation of the poems. The love poems are not 'about' Marguerite, nor are they actually about love; similarly the elegies are often not about the dead, whether people or faiths, nor even quite about transience and mutability as such. It is rather the poet's own self-conscious melancholy, aroused by reflection on these themes, that determines the emotional force and direction of these pieces. If the experience of love yielded the poet any positive conclusion, it was that at the moments of most intense communion with another, 'A man becomes aware of his life's flow',

> And then he thinks he knows
> The hills where his life rose
> And the sea where it goes. (291)

But even here, in 'The Buried Life', one of his more optimistic poems, the significance of the experience, its beneficiary, as it were, is a kind of reflective self-centredness. More generously, one might observe how much of Arnold's work, in prose as well as poetry, expresses his sustained, though not showily strenuous, search for self-knowledge. In a revealing letter to Clough, written in 1849 when still roused and disoriented by his love for 'Marguerite', he characterized himself as somebody 'whose one natural craving is not for profound thoughts, mighty spiritual workings etc etc but a distinct seeing of my way as far as my own nature is concerned' (C 110). This should remind us that, although Arnold is often taken as a representative of 'the Victorian crisis of faith' and similar large-scale intellectual shifts, he was not attempting to construct an alternative system or synthesis, in the way in which several

nineteenth-century doubters and self-declared 'humanists' were
trying to do; rather, more modestly, he was trying to 'see his way'.

But the more immediate conclusion to which the argument of
this chapter pushes us is to see that the voice of Arnold's poetry is
inherently reflexive: his poems are nearly always fundamentally
about himself, not just in the sense in which any artist's work is
the expression of something about himself, but rather in that, by a
series of covert mechanisms and sly stratagems, Arnold's poetry so
often contrives to make the mood and temperament of the poet
the focus of attention. Something of this was caught by Hutton
when, in another of his perceptive comments on Arnold's work, he
referred to the 'clear, self-contained, thoughtful, heroic egotism' of
much of the poetry. There *was* an element of heroism in Arnold's
struggle to come to terms with the intensity of his dissatisfaction,
but that, too, was egotistical, promoting to centre-stage the poet's
sensitivity and visible effort to accommodate himself to a grating
world.

This is surely partly accounted for by the deep but neglected
truth that melancholy is inescapably self-important, whereas there
is a relative impersonality about cheerfulness. Perhaps Arnold
arrived at an intuitive recognition of this truth; certainly, much of
the 'dialogue of the mind with itself' that took place in the early
1850s suggests an attempt to convince himself of the possibility of
rising to the level of cheerfulness, a development, as we shall see in
subsequent chapters, that he only really achieved, and then fitfully,
in his prose. In replying to Clough's favourable comments on 'The
Scholar-Gypsy', Arnold expressed his own dissatisfaction with the
merely self-indulgent aspect of his poetry.

I am glad you like the Gipsy Scholar—but what does it *do* for you? Homer
animates—Shakespeare *animates*—in its poor way I think Sohrab and
Rustum [Arnold's narrative poem of that name, first published in 1853]
animates—the Gipsy Scholar at best awakens a pleasing melancholy. But
this is not what we want.

> The complaining millions of men
> Darken in labour and pain—

[lines from his own 'The Youth of Nature'] what they want is something
to *animate* and *ennoble* them—not merely to add zest to their melancholy
or grace to their dreams. (C 146)

In the Preface to the 1853 volume of his poems (to be considered further in the next chapter), Arnold's curious repudiation of 'Empedocles on Etna' and the whole mood of anguished self-absorption he took it to represent, was part of his struggle to resist the charms of this 'pleasing melancholy'. That Preface was certainly not a successful way, and its programmatic recommendations stood at odds with Arnold's own best poetic practice. But he could not achieve in poetry what he recommended: it was not a register he commanded. When he tried to escape from himself to impersonal subjects like Nordic myth and Greek drama, he only succeeded in producing the lifeless husks of 'Balder Dead' and *Merope*. They are too willed: his gift did not run so far or so freely. In much of Arnold's poetry we see the disconsolate Romantic trying to turn himself into the resolute Stoic: his partial success has a pathos of its own, though we may wonder whether it is the small element of failure or the large degree of success which is the sadder sight. Yet there is a kind of self-indulgence here, too: genuine stoicism does not keep calling attention to its achievement in this way.

It is not the least of the reasons for which Arnold has been called 'the poet of our modernity' that this consuming self-consciousness was from the start allied to a note of precocious weariness. Although the theme of loss—loss of joy, loss of youth, loss of faith—is, as we have seen, at the heart of Arnold's lyrics and elegies, there is a sense in which what they register is absence rather than loss. That is, they mourn the fact that the poet—but also we, fellow-victims of history and the corrosion worked by its attendant self-consciousness—have never really known, can never know, the immediacy of real joy, real faith, or even—the precociousness returns in another role here—real youth. In a celebrated phrase, Arnold was later to charge that the Romantic poets were not 'adequate' to their age because, ultimately, they 'did not know enough' (iii. 262), but it could be said that his own poetry movingly expressed the existential plight of those upon whom history has imposed a choking burden of knowledge.

Increasingly, the loss of which he sang was the loss of the power of song itself. The drying-up of 'The fount that shall not flow again' (585) becomes just another of the grey truths to be, more in sorrow than in *angst*, accepted and lived with. The fact that 'the Muse be gone away' (578) was, as I suggested earlier, an enduring source of sadness to Arnold, and it left an undertow of regret and wistfulness occasionally discernible through the urbanity of the later prose. It is possible that he was for once overtly voicing this regret when he wrote of Sainte-Beuve's transition from an early dabbling in verse to his mature critical work:

Like so many who have tried their hand at *œuvres de poésie et d'art*, his preference, his dream, his ideal was there; the rest was comparatively journeyman-work, to be done well and estimably rather than ill and discreditably, and with precious rewards of its own, besides, in exercising the faculties and keeping off ennui; but still work of an inferior order. (v. 305)

But even if Arnold did share this feeling, his own objectivity led him immediately to deny that Sainte-Beuve would have been justified in this self-assessment, given the immense value of his critical *œuvre* set alongside the work of even some of the most creative writers of his time. In the following chapters I shall try to show that, despite the undeniable, if patchy, glories of his poetry, *our* objectivity requires that, whatever sadness it may have brought to Arnold himself, we cannot regret that the greater part of his achievement was to be in prose.

4 The literary critic

It is his work as a critic, more than anything else, that has earned Arnold his pedestal among the immortals. Naturally, there has been a good deal of wailing and lamenting that his emergence as a critic should have been accompanied by—whether as cause or consequence has teased biographers ever since—the drying up of his poetic gift; but he would, without question, cut a smaller figure today had he never turned to criticism, and through his precept and his example he has exercised an enduring and unrivalled influence over the place of criticism in our culture. T. S. Eliot's famous observation that Arnold was 'rather a propagandist for criticism than a critic' was ungenerous on several counts, not least because Eliot's cultural criticism owed much to Arnold: the implied judgement is too dismissive of Arnold's actual criticism, while 'propagandist' is too redolent of a loudspeakerly dogmatism to do justice to the sinuous suggestiveness of Arnold's essays. There was tendentiousness of a different kind in the remark by F. R. Leavis, another critic to feel the length of Arnold's shadow, that Arnold's 'best work is that of a literary critic even when it is not literary criticism'. But we do not have to accede to the restrictive notion of 'literary criticism' underlying Leavis's comment any more than we have to endorse the terms of Eliot's judgement to recognize that, taken together, these two remarks provide a helpful orientation to the true nature of Arnold's achievement. It is on account of what he did *for* criticism as much as what he did *in* it that we value him, while, conversely, we are aware that the qualities he brought to the wide range of subjects he treated were pre-eminently the qualities of an outstanding literary critic.

Modernity and 'the Grand Style'

Every poet is a critic of poetry. The practice of the craft impels an awareness of the possible uses of the resources of form and language, and where this is combined with an intelligent interest in the work of one's predecessors and contemporaries, there is criticism going on though a line of prose never be written. In this sense, Arnold was a critic from the start. His letters to Clough in the late 1840s constitute a playful, informal seminar on poetic theory. He stands out, with self-conscious sternness, against the Keatsian tradition in early Victorian verse, with its rich abundance of imagery and lush word-pictures but also its lack of large controlling ideas or proper elevation of tone. By way of a corrective, he turns to his favourite classical authors and their English descendants. 'There are', he responds to Clough in a letter of 1849,

two offices of Poetry—one to add to one's store of thoughts and feelings— another to compose and elevate the mind by a sustained tone, numerous allusions, and a grand style. What other process is Milton's than this last, in Comus for instance? . . . Nay in Sophocles what is valuable is not so much his contributions to psychology and the anatomy of sentiment, as the grand moral effects produced by *style*. For the style is the expression of the nobility of the poet's character, as the matter is the expression of the richness of his mind: but on men character produces as great an effect as mind. (C 100-1)

These precociously grave observations (Arnold was 26) contain the germ of much of his later critcism.

The severe reaction against what he took to be the inhibiting reflectiveness of some of his earlier poetry—the reaction that led him to omit 'Empedocles on Etna' from his *Poems* of 1853—also provoked his first statement of poetical principles in the Preface to that volume. The somewhat mannered, exaggeratedly olympian tone of the piece was a further expression of that wilful serenity which had already irritated some of his contemporaries ('I admire Matt—to a very great extent,' wrote the future historian J. A. Froude to Clough: 'Only I don't see what business he has to parade his calmness and lecture us on resignation when he has never known what a storm is, and doesn't know what he has to resign himself to. . . .'). The Preface calls for a return to the themes of the Ancients: the great primary affections and their expression in noble actions. A young writer's attention (the author of this greybeard advice was now 30) 'should be fixed on excellent models that he may reproduce, at any rate, something of their excellence, by penetrating himself with their works and by catching their spirit. . . .' (i. 8–9). Their great quality, he ruled, is 'sanity', and therefore (as he restated his point the following year) 'it is impossible to read carefully the great Ancients, without losing something of our caprice and eccentricity' (i. 17). The central insistence of his mature criticism on the need for 'centrality' as a corrective to the provincial and the eccentric is already evident here. He adumbrates another theme of his later criticism, as well as revealing an abiding reservation about Shakespeare, when he remarked that the latter 'has not the severe and scrupulous self-restraint of the Ancients, partly, no doubt, because he had a far less cultivated and exacting audience' (i. 11).

The 1853 Preface has a particular biographical interest, both as a repudiation of aspects of a former poetic self, and as Arnold's first public engagement in those critical controversies that were to be the stimulus to his best work. Implicitly, it was a lofty dismissal of those Keatsian epigoni slightingly referred to as the 'Spasmodic' school of lyric poets. But, as with his own experiments with classical poetic forms and subjects in the 1850s, his prose writings of this decade reveal him trying on certain doctrines and tones, searching for a voice in which to express his prematurely Stoic withdrawal from the empty bustle of modern society.

His inaugural lecture as Professor of Poetry at Oxford, 'On The Modern Element in Literature' (which he delivered in 1857 but did not publish until 1869, and which, significantly, he never republished), saw him adopting a more historical approach. At least, it was ostensibly historical, with much talk of the development of society in different periods, yet in fact the argument of the lecture rests on ahistorical typology and deliberate anachronism. That argument, which perhaps owed something to his father's cyclical view of history, was that the present age needed to be brought to recognize its special affinity with the literature of those other ages which could also be characterized as 'modern', that is, ages which were 'culminating epochs', which exhibited a 'significant spectacle' in themselves and which sought for an 'adequate' literature as a means of comprehending that spectacle. Predictably, especially at this point in Arnold's development, the two candidates for this

status which he considers are Greece and Rome. The latter, however, though a 'highly modern' and 'deeply significant' epoch,
did not produce an 'adequate' literature, and so the resounding
conclusion of the inaugural lecture by the first holder of the Chair
to break with tradition and deliver his lecture in English (rather
than in Latin) was to 'establish the absolute, the enduring interest
of Greek literature, and, above all, of Greek poetry' (i. 37).

This lecture and the Preface to his verse-drama *Merope*, published in the following year, represent the classicizing tendency in
Arnold's aesthetic at its highest pitch. Their cultivated remoteness
from the concerns of his own society was regarded as affected
antiquarianism, though it in fact expressed, albeit in a displaced
form, an absorbing antagonism to some of the features of that
society's sensibility. In retrospect, we may discern a close connection between the facts that Arnold had yet to find his own prose
voice and that he had still to engage more directly with the cultural
preoccupations of his contemporaries. Ironically, he was to do both
these things by turning to the most distant point in the Western
tradition, the poetry of Homer.

On Translating Homer

Although the three lectures that Arnold published in 1861 under
the title *On Translating Homer* are festooned with allusions to long-
forgotten controversies about an already arcane subject, this slim
volume, together with its pamphlet sequel *Last Words*, remains
an impressive and surprisingly accessible statement of the indispensable role of critical judgement and tact even, perhaps
especially, in matters where technical scholarship may seem to
exercise unchallengeable authority. The middle of the nineteenth
century saw an unusual concentration of attempts at that per-
ennially fascinating task of rendering Homer into English. The
greatest claim on posterity's attention now exercised by either
Ichabod Charles Wright or F. W. Newman (brother of the theologian) is as authors of the translations that furnished the chief
butts for Arnold's witty criticisms. Indeed, some readers, both
then and since, have judged Arnold too funny by half, and have

regretted that his statement of critical principles should have appeared in this polemical form. But it is arguable that this misconstrues Arnold's purpose, as well as perhaps failing to recognize the role of such controversy in setting his mind in motion. No writer can be entirely indifferent to the anticipated verdict of posterity, but the cultural critic, to take only the most relevant category, necessarily has a more immediate audience primarily in mind. Arnold well knew that his 'vivacities' were a calculated risk, but he was convinced that his was a more effective way of gaining the ear and winning the heart of his contemporary English readers than through more solemn and systematic statement. Moreover, the movement of his own mind was—to call upon a still useful sense of an over-used word—dialectical. He needed to have a one-sided or exaggerated view to correct in order to be stirred to articulate his own more complex sense of a truth.

There is far more in these lectures than destructive criticism, but they undeniably contain some destructive criticism of a very high order. He was unsparing on the failings of translators who are deaf to the subtler literary qualities of the original, and he was brilliantly effective in showing how preconceptions derived from historical learning produced misapprehensions of rhythm and poetic effect. High among Arnold's targets was what might be called the pedantry of authenticity, those various ways in which a misplaced fidelity to the assumed conditions of an earlier period can hamstring creative interpretation in the present. For example, he observed of Newman's theory that, because the dialect of Homer was itself archaic, the translator should confine his vocabulary as far as possible to the elements in the language of Anglo-Saxon origin:

Such a theory seems to me both dangerous for a translator and false in itself. Dangerous for a translator, because wherever one finds such a theory announced . . . it is generally followed by an explosion of pedantry, and pedantry is of all things in the world the most un-Homeric. False in itself, because, in fact, we owe to the Latin element in our language most of that very rapidity and clear decisiveness by which it is contradistinguished from the German, and in sympathy with the languages of Greece and Rome; so that to limit an English translator of Homer to words of Saxon origin is to deprive him of one of his special advantages for translating Homer. (i. 101)

There was a similar realism and good sense in his response to the proposal that the familiar, and for Arnold and his readers deeply resonant, forms of Greek names should be changed to correspond with a more 'correct' transliteration in the hope that this would come to seem natural to the next generation:

For my part, I feel no disposition to pass all my own life in the wilderness of pedantry, in order that a posterity which I shall never see may one day enter an orthographical Canaan; and, after all, the real question is this: whether our living apprehension of the Greek world is more checked by meeting in an English book about the Greeks, names not spelt letter for letter as in the original Greek, or by meeting names which make us rub our eyes and call out, 'How exceedingly odd!' (i. 150)

More importantly, Newman and his fellow-offenders were for Arnold symptomatic of something much deeper. 'The eccentricity, . . . the arbitrariness of which Mr Newman's conception of Homer offers so signal an example, are not a peculiar failing of Mr Newman's own; in varying degrees they are the great defect of English intellect, the great blemish of English literature' (i. 140). Whereas in Europe 'the main effort, for now many years, has been a *critical* effort; the endeavour, in all branches of knowledge— theology, philosophy, history, art, science—to see the object as in itself it really is', the play of criticism, in this wide sense, has been, he alleged, notably lacking in England. *On Translating Homer* was the first instalment of Arnold's emerging programme to bring some of this critical light to bear on the benighted attitudes of his countrymen. Actually, some of the most telling points were made in the pamphlet which he published in response to Newman's reply to his original criticisms. Newman lodged numerous complaints against both the tone and substance of Arnold's lectures, not all of them unjustified. But his final accusation allowed Arnold a reply in his most provoking manner, in the course of which he gave a marvellously perceptive account of the perennial obstacles to good criticism:

And he ends by saying that my ignorance is great. Alas! that is very true. Much as Mr Newman was mistaken when he talked of my rancour, he is entirely right when he talks of my ignorance. And yet, perverse as it seems to say so, I sometimes find myself wishing, when dealing with these matters of poetical criticism, that my ignorance were even greater than it is. To handle these matters properly there is needed a poise so perfect that the least overweight in any direction tends to destroy the balance. Temper destroys it, a crotchet destroys it, even erudition may destroy it. To press to the sense of the thing itself with which one is dealing, not to go off on some collateral issue about the thing, is the hardest matter in the world. The 'thing itself' with which one is here dealing, the critical perception of poetic truth—is of all things the most volatile, elusive, and evanescent; by even pressing too impetuously after it, one runs the risk of losing it. The critic of poetry should have the finest tact, the nicest moderation, the most free, flexible, and elastic spirit imaginable.

This passage is a good example of the way Arnold's mind moves from an intuitive perception of the lack of balance in an apparently unexceptionable thought to a widely-ramifying articulation of the basis of that intuition. His tone is initially ironic and personal, but the weight of the argument itself pulls it into a more serious and impersonal register. The unfolding of the implications of that quint-essentially Arnoldian term 'poise' has a persuasive momentum. Temper destroys the crucial balance because through the fumes of his own emotion the critic can see nothing as in itself it really is; a crotchet—that is, a pet theory or idiosyncratic preoccupation— destroys it because the critic is inevitably looking for evidence of what he wants to see, he is obsessed with his theory rather than responding to the object of critical attention; then that splendid culminating clause, 'even erudition may destroy it', that is, that the critic may become so absorbed in points of historical or philological detail, that he loses all sense of proportion, and his learning, instead of serving as a helpful auxiliary, obstructs his appreciation of the poem as a whole. And finally the insight, itself an expression of poise, that the 'critical perception of poetic truth' is so 'volatile, elusive, and evanescent' that 'by even pressing too impetuously after it, one runs the risk of losing it'. This surely catches very well that sense, itself elusive and evanescent, that when we press to try to grasp the nature of some complex literary experience, we run the risk of somehow driving it away, or prematurely fixing on a description which is, in fact, inadequate and hence distorting. He is pointing to the way that we have, in some sense, to let the experience come to us a little more, and then to enter and explore its dimensions in a meditative, noticing sort of way, rather than rushing to try to pin it down. And here again we should feel the force of that deceptively simple Arnoldian injunction to try to see the object as in *itself* it *really* is.

Criticism and its functions

The fact that *Essays in Criticism* (1865) now seems such a coherent book, despite its origin as a collection of lectures and periodical pieces from the preceding two or three years, is testimony to, among other things, the constancy of polemical purpose that animated Arnold in these years. Actually, coherence is not what first strikes the reader on looking at the contents page. The first edition of the book contained nine essays and a specially-written preface: two of the essays are the subsequently famous general statements 'The Function of Criticism at the Present Time' and 'The Literary Influence of Academies'; of the remaining seven, three deal with relatively minor French authors (Maurice de Guérin, Eugénie de Guérin, Joubert) and there is one each on Heine, Spinoza, Marcus Aurelius, and 'Pagan and Mediaeval Religious Sentiment'. In other words, one of the most famous works of literary criticism in the English language appears to contain much that would not now be regarded as 'literature', very little on indisputably significant authors, and nothing at all on any literature in English. But there is a unity to it, and as so often with Arnold one can best grasp this by looking at the way the essays developed in response to the controversies he was engaged in.

The starting-point is an essay that did not appear in this form in the book at all. In 1862, the Anglican Bishop of Natal, J. W. Colenso, published the first instalment of his *The Pentateuch and Book of Joshua Critically Examined*, a work which sparked off one of those now-forgotten storms that shook the Victorian church. Colenso questioned the plausibility of certain passages of the Bible if interpreted literally, as for many their faith still obliged them to do. Arnold might have been sympathetic to this enterprise had it been carried out with more finesse and tact, but these were hardly Colenso's distinguishing qualities. To make the point, Arnold conceived the plan of contrasting Colenso's 'jejune and technical manner of dealing with Biblical controversy with that of Spinoza in his famous treatise on the *Interpretation of Scripture*' (L i. 204). (Spinoza had long been one of Arnold's favourite authors; some passages from this initial article were to be reused in the one that eventually appeared in *Essays in Criticism* under the title 'Spinoza and the Bible'.) What it was about Colenso's absurdly reductionist calculations that so irked Arnold is easily gleaned from the following specimens of the Higher Knockabout: Colenso's mathematical demonstrations are, as Arnold described them,

a series of problems, the solution of each of which is meant to be the *reductio ad absurdum* of that Book of the Pentateuch which supplied its terms. . . . For example, . . . as to the account in Leviticus of the provision made for the priests: '*If three priests have to eat 264 pigeons a day, how many must each priest eat?*' That disposes of Leviticus. . . . For Deuteronomy, take the number of lambs slain at the Sanctuary, as compared with the space for slaying them: '*In an area of 1692 square yards, how many lambs per minute can 150,000 persons kill in two hours?*' Certainly not 1250, the number required, and the Book of Deuteronomy, therefore, shares the fate of its predecessors. (iii. 48)

But what really disturbed Arnold and prompted him to ridicule the already ridiculous was the extent to which Colenso was taken seriously by large sections of educated opinion in England. This demonstrated yet again the parochialism of English intellectual life, the want of those standards of critical judgement by which such an eccentric performance could be properly judged. And this meant, Arnold insisted, pursuing his larger purpose, being judged not simply from a theological point of view, but 'before another tribunal', that of what he called 'literary criticism'. But what business, he asks rhetorically, has literary criticism with books on religious matters? His answer is worth quoting *in extenso*, because though he was to refine his statement of the tasks of criticism, no other passage reveals so clearly the ideal animating his larger critical campaigns.

Literary criticism's most important function is to try books as to the influence which they are calculated to have upon the general culture of single nations or of the world at large. Of this culture literary criticism is the appointed guardian, and on this culture all literary works may be conceived as in some way or other operating. All these works have a special professional criticism to undergo: theological works that of theologians, historical works that of historians, philosophical works that of philosophers, and in this case each kind of work is tried by a separate standard. But they have also a general literary criticism to undergo, and this tries them all, as I have said, by one standard—their effect upon general culture. Everyone is not a theologian, a historian, or a philosopher, but everyone is interested in the advance in the general culture of his nation or of mankind. A criticism, therefore, which, abandoning a thousand special questions which may be raised about any book, tries it solely in respect of its influence upon this culture, brings it thereby within the sphere of everyone's interest. (iii. 41)

At first sight, this may appear to be another of those pieces of intellectual imperialism whereby the proponent of one discipline attempts to assert its sovereignty over neighbouring intellectual territories. But it should be clear that Arnold was not writing on behalf of the academic practice we have come to know as 'literary criticism'. He was, to begin with, using 'literary' in a very wide sense: works of theology, history, or philosophy are, in this now somewhat archaic sense, all branches of 'literature'. But an ambitious sense of 'criticism' is involved, too. He does not, after all, say that literary criticism is qualified to discriminate or assess some purely *literary* qualities of these works; he says the 'most important function' of criticism is to 'try books as to the influence which they are calculated to have upon the general culture'. No small task: above all, not a task for the specialist, or even a team of specialists. It requires the exercise of cultivated judgement, formed by responsive engagement with work of the highest standard. 'Literary criticism' is the name Arnold was here giving to this task of general judgement.

These large claims predictably provoked indignation and hostility from several quarters, which may have hardened Arnold in his already exaggerated conviction that genuine criticism was unknown and unwelcome in England. The essays which he wrote between 1862 and 1864, and which were then collected in *Essays in Criticism*, were intended both as a direct response to these objections and as a demonstration of the role of criticism in practice, while the choice of subject-matter was meant to supply another lack by encouraging a more discriminating appreciation of just those writers and cultural traditions likely to be scorned or undervalued in mid-Victorian England.

Arnold generalized his case in the two essays he placed at the head of his collection, which have become two of the most frequently cited pieces he ever wrote. It is in the first, 'The Function of Criticism at the Present Time', that we meet his famous definition of criticism as 'the disinterested endeavour to learn and propagate the best that is known and thought in the world'. His explanation of that crucial Arnoldian word 'disinterested' is worth pondering for a moment, especially since it has come in for more than its share of misunderstanding.

And how is criticism to show disinterestedness? By keeping aloof from what is called 'the practical view of things'; by resolutely following the law of its own nature, which is to be a free play of the mind on all subjects which it touches. By steadily refusing to lend itself to any of those ulterior, political, practical considerations about ideas, which plenty of people will be sure to attach to them, which in this country at any rate are certain to be attached to them quite sufficiently, but which criticism really has nothing to do with. (iii. 270)

It is true that this is one of those passages that collaborate in their own misinterpretation, but in the context of the essay as a whole it should be clear that Arnold is *not* claiming that criticism exists in some transcendental sphere, unconnected with the social and political realities of the world; if he were, his whole programme for the impact of criticism upon that world would be absurd. Nor is he claiming that the critic has no political, religious, or moral values, or that he is uninterested in the relation of the objects of his criticism to those values—'disinterested' does not, it ought to be unnecessary to say, mean 'uninterested'.

What Arnold is attacking here is any attempt to subordinate criticism to some other purpose. The aim of criticism, as he had already insisted more than once, is 'to see the object as in itself it really is', and that means not immediately and primarily responding to a book or idea in terms of whether its consequences may be acceptable by the criteria of some moral or religious or political view which we are already committed to, but trying first to let it register on our minds and sensibilities in the fullest ways possible, trying to let its own nature manifest itself to us without prematurely foreclosing on whether it is or is not acceptable in terms of a standard imported from some other sphere. Arnold's reference in that passage to the situation in England gives the clue to what he was trying to avoid. Those 'ulterior, political, practical considerations about ideas' that he is urging criticism to keep aloof from were precisely the kinds of habits that, in his view, narrowed and stultified the intellectual life of Victorian England. Books and ideas were judged, he was complaining, by whether they were consistent with the true tenets of the Protestant religion, or by whether they supported a Whig or Tory view of the English constitution, or by whether they had an immediate bearing upon the great policy issues of the moment. By urging the critic to practise a kind of 'disinterestedness', he was not encouraging a posture of withdrawal from the world, but rather that kind of openness that is not so blinded by partisan preconceptions that it cannot recognize a new idea or appreciate a new form when it meets it.

It is certainly arguable that Arnold himself did not always live up to this ideal in practice, so committed was he to promoting a particular set of changes in English sensibilities; he could be unfair and tendentious in his own ways, and he sometimes takes that kind of self-conscious pleasure in his own verbal felicity that is itself an obstacle to the truly disinterested treatment of a subject. But to an impressive extent Arnold *did* successfully embody this quality; certainly by the standards of the literary journalism of his day (as exhibited in, for example, the political propagandizing and hanging-judge severity of the *Edinburgh* and *Quarterly* reviews), his criticism was remarkably free from partisan spirit, and it can still communicate a sense of spaciousness and long perspectives. And, of course, some of his choices revealed that kind of disinterestedness which is akin to courage, especially when his subjects challenged some of the entrenched prejudices of his society, as, for example, in elevating Marcus Aurelius over his Christian detractors as a model of 'spiritual refinement', or in writing such an enthusiastic appreciation of Joubert, whom he called 'the French Coleridge', when he knew that Joubert, as an enlightened Frenchman, would probably be suspected by the English public of atheism, materialism, levity, and syphilis.

The second essay, 'The Literary Influence of Academies', has also come in for its share of misinterpretation. It is often described as a lament about the absence in England of an authoritative institution comparable to the French *Académie française*. But this way of putting it then seems to bring us up against the following paradox in Arnold's views about criticism. As we have seen, one of the general terms he uses most frequently to characterize the distinctive qualities of criticism in his sense is 'flexibility'. But it is the essence of the idea of an Academy that it should be authoritative, and indeed, where its pronouncements are made *ex cathedra*, that it should be somewhat authoritarian. 'Rigidity' rather than 'flexibility' might seem to be the quality an Academy would be most likely to foster. How, therefore, was Arnold able to recommend both these things simultaneously?

Although this question does point to an enduring tension in Arnold's mind between two not entirely compatible inclinations, the tension falls some way short of a genuine contradiction in this case. To begin with, we have to recognize that Arnold was *not* in fact recommending the establishment of an Academy in England. Rather, he was trying to highlight the weaknesses of English intellectual life and literature by contrasting them with the qualities encouraged by, and in fact expressed in, the existence of an authoritative institution like an Academy. The very existence of an Academy along the lines of the *Académie française* expresses a public recognition of the importance of maintaining the highest standards in any sphere of intellectual activity. As Arnold makes clear, he is not talking about works of genius: the English were, he argued, already too prone to compliment themselves on having Shakespeare, Milton, and a string of great poets, and so complacently to conclude that the conditions for literary and intellectual achievement in their country must be in pretty good order. But that is not the point; individuals of genius, especially in a genre like poetry, may appear from time to time, without the general culture of the society being in good order at all. What about what Arnold calls the 'journey-man work of literature' (in the wide sense of that latter term), that is, the work of reviewing and journalism, of translation, reference, and biography? He gives some telling examples of how poorly this was done in England, and then observes:

Ignorance and charlatanism in work of this kind are always trying to pass off their wares as excellent, and to cry down criticism as the voice of an insignificant, over-fastidious minority; they easily persuade the multitude that this is so when the minority is scattered about as it is here; not so easily when it is banded together as it is in the French Academy. (iii. 242)

Again, we see his concern to make criticism effective and to combat that ethos of lax relativism which allows every opinion, no matter how eccentric or ill-grounded, to pass itself off as the equal of any other. Notice, too, his reference to the opposition between the minority and the multitude, in fact the assumption of an antagonistic relation between them. This raises the interesting question (to which I shall return in a slightly different form later) of how Arnold squares his recognition of the fact that the business of culture will in the first instance be carried on by a minority, or as he calls them elsewhere, adopting a biblical phrase, 'the saving remnant', with his claim that disinterested judgement can only proceed from a position of cultural centrality. Can a 'remnant' be 'central'?

In fact, this very notion of 'cultural centrality' itself points toward a deeper resolution of our initial paradox about the conflict between flexibility and authoritativeness. The opposite of an open and flexible mind is, of course, a closed and rigid one, but there are many ways of being closed and rigid. The particular way that Arnold intends is where one is a prisoner of a narrow, partisan, obsessive point of view, where one is confined within the limits of a parochial preoccupation, a provincial standard of judgement, a purely personal range of reference. In this sense, to be brought to participate in the mainstream of European culture is to be emancipated from the constraints of provincial narrowness, and to have access to the highest standards is to be liberated from the despotism of the mediocre and second-rate. In contrasting the eccentric, wayward, opinionated quality of much English prose with the classical lucidity and restraint of the best French writers, Arnold cites a passage from the French writer Bossuet and says: 'There we have prose without the note of provinciality—classical prose, prose of the centre' (iii. 246). That reference to prose of 'the centre' is crucial, and very revealing of the shape of Arnold's concerns in this essay. To be central in this sense is, if you like, to operate within the largest space; the contrast is the way in which one is cramped if confined just to the margin or periphery. Arnold, then, is not recommending the establishment of an Academy in

England: he is trying to bring out how the strengths of a culture that can create and sustain an Academy are precisely the kinds of qualities most lacking in England. He is not so much saying that English intellectual life exhibits such a low level and a lack of standards because it does not have an Academy, but rather that, because of the qualities manifested in its low level and its lack of standards, it could never understand the virtues of having an Academy in the first place.

In 1865 Arnold prefaced his collection with a high-spirited response to some of the criticisms that had accumulated over the previous three or four years. Actually, the Preface which now (since the second edition of 1869) stands at the front of the volume is a considerably toned-down version of the original. In the first edition, he indulged his taste for making his critics look ridiculous while artfully retaining the reader's sympathy for himself. 'It will make you laugh', he told his mother (L i. 286), but it didn't, and he had sadly to recognize that 'from their training and habits of thinking and feeling' his family were unlikely to appreciate some of his immoderate sallies (iii. 482). Nor were many of his other readers very appreciative of the facetious mockery of Arnold's minor Dunciad. *The North British Review* was typical in objecting to what, in a term that was to stick, it called Arnold's 'vivacities' ('but then', as he explained to his mother, 'it is a Scotchman who writes' [L i. 290]). For all his confident swagger, Arnold soon realized that the tone of his raillery could be counter-productive, and thereafter omitted some of the offending passages. Still, it remains one of the least dull Prefaces to a work of criticism ever written, and as a counterpoint to the coarse practicality of some of his Benthamite critics, it concludes with his famous aria to the charms of Oxford, 'steeped in sentiment as she lies, spreading her gardens to the moonlight, and whispering from her towers the last enchantments of the Middle Age' (iii. 290).

Although, as I have suggested, it was controversy that brought Arnold's mind to life at this period, the volume we hold in our hands today as *Essays in Criticism, First Series* (the suffix was added by the publishers after Arnold's death in 1888 when they collected some of his later pieces, as he had been planning to do, under the title *Essays in Criticism, Second Series*) is remarkably free from disfiguring birth-scars. The volume has idiosyncrasies of its own, to be sure. Arnold's typically nineteenth-century method of reproducing very long extracts from his authors without much comment is apt to seem tiresome (and to raise ungenerous thoughts about reviewers who are paid by length). In fact, this practice makes us aware how little there is in the book of what we now generally regard as the distinctive activity of the literary critic, the close attention to the way in which the language of particular passages works; Arnold, here true to his late-Romantic pedigree, was always better at characterizing *what* effect a work has upon the reader than he was at analysing *how* that effect is achieved. As a result, we are sometimes left wondering why what may seem to us a rather laboured passage is being held up for our admiration: Arnold's method is very vulnerable to changes of taste in this respect. Certainly, the de Guérins, for example, now seem inadequate vehicles for the case he wants to make. This owed something to following the taste of his admired Sainte-Beuve too closely, perhaps, but it also brings out how some of the writing in these essays is less a response to the authors in question, and more a matter of using those authors to illustrate an argument about the nature of criticism.

At times, too, the essays seem to be marked by thumpingly dogmatic judgements (for example, this piece of unfairness to Jeffrey, first editor of *The Edinburgh Review*: 'All his vivacity and accomplishments avail him nothing; of the true critic he had in an eminent degree no quality, except one — curiosity' [iii. 210]). But these dicta are almost invariably a way of establishing a larger, comparative point. In order to show up and correct the eccentricity of English taste, Arnold constantly invokes the wider frame of judgement provided by comparison: his preoccupation with 'ranking' authors, with assigning them their proper place in the league tables of literary greatness, which was later to become a disfiguring tic, here simply takes its place as part of his overall strategy. That strategy, as we have seen, was not a modest one: in Arnold's sense of the term, criticism took all human knowledge as its province, where 'its best spiritual work', as he put it, was 'to keep man from a self-satisfaction which is retarding and vulgarising' (iii, 271). In

the end, what gives *Essays in Criticism* a surprising unity and coherence is the presence in each essay of the idea of criticism itself,
embodied in that distinctive Arnoldian voice. 'The great art of
criticism is to get oneself out of the way and to let humanity decide'
(iii. 227). Arnold could hardly be said always to have lived up to
this injunction, so recognizable, so much a personality of its own,
was that voice. But it accompanied rather than drowned its
subject-matter. Here, he admirably embodied his own ideal: the
critic, he observed in a passage which catches the spirit of the book
very sweetly, should not always be delivering judgements, but
should endeavour rather to be communicating what he sees to the
reader 'and letting his own judgment .pass along with it—but
insensibly, and in the second place not the first, as a sort of companion and clue, not as an abstract lawgiver' (iii. 283).

Later literary essays

Apart from the curious little book of lectures *On The Study of
Celtic Literature*, published in 1867, which was more an essay in
the comparative analysis of national character than about Celtic
literature as such, Arnold published little of note on literary
matters for twelve years after *Essays in Criticism*. During that time
he was largely absorbed in the social and religious criticism which
forms the subject-matter of the next two chapters. When in the
last decade of his life he did again return to literary topics, his sense
both of the task and the audience had changed somewhat. In the
early 1860s he had, with pardonable exaggeration, felt himself to
be struggling to obtain for criticism any kind of hearing at all; by
the late 1870s he felt the need to distance himself from the 'historical' and 'aesthetic' schools of criticism then growing up. Again,
in his earlier criticism he had dealt almost exclusively with classical
and European literature, calling the narrowness of English taste
before the bar of the highest cosmopolitan standards; in the essays
of his last decade he returned more and more to establishing the
canon of English classics, self-consciously revising and completing
the work of Dr Johnson, impelled above all by the urge to settle
accounts with the great masters of English Romanticism whose
literary stepchild he was. And finally, his sense of the relevant

audience had changed too: in his earlier work he had been addressing that minority which shared a classical education and read the quarterly and monthly periodicals, whereas from the late 1870s he was aware that the changed educational and social circumstances of Britain in the last quarter of the nineteenth century were creating a far wider market for a certain sort of instruction and moral sustenance.

These changes, acting in conjunction with the darker colours assumed by Arnold's own sorrow-shadowed sensibilities, gave his later work a more didactic and moralistic tone. The easy, conversational intimacy of the earlier work became less marked, though it never entirely disappeared; instead, the greater distance and inequality between author and implied reader produced a more insistent and preachy literary manner. As Arnold himself increasingly required his reading to console rather than to animate, he entrusted literature with the heavy duty of making the truths of religion and morality effective. The essays on Wordsworth, Byron, Keats, and Gray, which all originated as introductions to popular editions of selections of their poetry, still contain some interesting criticism (especially that on Wordsworth), but they are not his best work. It is particularly unfortunate that the most widely anthologized of all of Arnold's prose writings should have been the programmatic essay on 'The Study of Poetry', written as a general introduction to T. H. Ward's popular compilation *The English Poets* (and hence addressed to a relatively unsophisticated audience), since it displays these characteristics of his last period in their most marked form.

It is in this essay that he expounds his famous doctrine of the 'touchstones', those lines of indisputably great poetry (from Homer or Dante, Shakespeare or Milton) that we should bring to the task of helping us discriminate between good and bad poetry, and indeed between great and merely good poetry. This approach has come in for severe, and largely justified, criticism: abstracting single lines from complex poetic wholes is an exercise fraught with pitfalls, just as there are obvious difficulties about comparing these lines with poetry of different genres or written in different languages, and so on. But Arnold was not in fact proposing this as a complete scholarly method (he was not writing at that level), and his own account of the value of this approach is more modest:

Indeed, there can be no more useful help for discovering what poetry belongs to the class of the truly excellent, and can therefore do us most good, than to have always in one's mind lines and expressions of the great masters, and to apply them as a touchstone to other poetry. Of course we are not to require this other poetry to resemble them; it may be very dissimilar. But if we have any tact we shall find them, when we have lodged them well in our minds, an infallible touchstone for detecting the presence or absence of high poetic quality, and also the degree of this quality, in all other poetry which we may place beside them. (ix. 168)

Once again, 'critical tact' is indispensable; the touchstones can, of course, be applied clumsily and mechanically, but any critical approach can be travestied when it falls into clumsy and mechanical hands. The touchstones are, as this passage says, only a 'help' for discovering the quality of a given piece of poetry, not a sufficient recipe in themselves. But they have the effect of disciplining our taste: in their presence it becomes impossible to be taken in by the fraudulent and second-rate; the contrast jars our sensibilities too much. Arnold had himself deployed essentially this approach at various times in his Homer lectures, as well as in *Essays in Criticism*: in this essay, the touchstones are simply being proffered as the handy pocket-version of the Arnoldian conception of criticism.

But in that passage about the touchstones there was a single word which encapsulated the later Arnold's argument about the high function to be assigned to literature. 'There can be no more useful help for discovering what poetry belongs to the class of the truly excellent, and can *therefore* [my emphasis] do us most good . . .'. This raises several questions—what kind of 'good' does poetry do us? why does the best poetry do us the most good?—but at the heart of the connection Arnold is asserting lies the question of arousing the feelings or sentiments. He is, that is to say, not so much concerned with questions about how we *decide* what is right and wrong—like so many of his contemporaries, he thought the answers to those questions were for the most part not obscure or in doubt—but rather with how we are to become the kind of person who habitually and spontaneously *does* what is right, how we discipline our will, how we overcome selfishness, laziness, doubt, and

despair. In Arnold's view, it is precisely the opposite of these negative states that poetry, above all other agencies, fosters in us. Put
very briefly, his view is that poetry (by which he means literature
in general, though he always gives pride of place to poetry in the
narrow sense) can not only express these convictions, but can give
them such beauty or power that they act on our emotions and thus
arouse or console us in a way that mere philosophical statement of
them cannot do. The better the poetry, the more effectively it
engages our emotions and stirs us to action, and the more, therefore, we become the *kinds* of people that it is morally desirable we
should become. And a crucial part of this, especially in Arnold's
later writings, is the way the most noble or elevated poetry *reconciles*
us to the universe, gives us that kind of consolation that can make
existence seem bearable.

This is the thought that informs the famous opening sentence of
the essay: 'The future of poetry is immense, because in poetry,
where it is worthy of its high destinies, our race, as time goes on,
will find an ever surer and surer stay' (ix. 161). 'Stay' aptly suggests
the propping-up of something otherwise doomed to crumble (and
thus also calls up the opening line of his early sonnet 'Who prop,
thou ask'st, in these bad days, my mind?' [110], which famously
assigns Sophocles this role). Literature is to console and sustain us
in hard times, with the strong implication that life is mostly hard
times. (The relation with his religious thought will become apparent in Chapter 6 below; here we may simply note that the first
paragraph of this essay ends 'The strongest part of our religion
today is its unconscious poetry'.) Thus alerted, we notice how the
touchstones themselves are nearly all lines that express a melancholy or stoic mood, a certain noble resignation in the face of
the universe; and this is the dominant note of his late essays.

Arnold had his limitations as a critic; so many, in fact, especially
in his later work, that his inclusion in the pantheon of criticism can
sometimes seem puzzling. To begin with, his tastes were severely
traditional and in some ways surprisingly narrow. The classics cast
too long a shadow: no subsequent literature could match them,
and this can sometimes give a note of slightly chilly disdain to his
judgements of recent authors, certainly a lack of enthusiasm. He
was not above treating experiment and innovation as wilful neglect

of 'the best that has been thought and said'; and with the best always in the past, and a pretty distant past at that, he could seem to be inflexibly judging later literature by (as it has nicely been put) 'doomsday standards'. Further, he consistently under-appreciated all the lighter genres. He lauded tragedy, but never did justice to comedy—indeed, scarcely paid attention to it in his major critical manifestos. He prized the epic above all forms of poetry, but undervalued wit and satire. In not regarding the Meta-physical Poets of the seventeenth century as a major moment of English poetry he was, of course, only sharing the received Vic-torian view, but share it he did; a greater critic might have revised it (as T. S. Eliot was to do). Similarly, he had a late-Romantic aversion to what he regarded as the mere polish and artificiality of the Augustans; he dismissively (but memorably) declared of Dry-den and Pope that they 'are not classics of our poetry; they are classics of our prose' (ix. 181). He disparaged Chaucer; and has any English critic of standing written so little or so poorly about Shakespeare?

Then, apart from one very late essay on Tolstoy (which was chiefly an exposition of *Anna Karenina* and an assessment of his moral teaching), Arnold almost entirely neglected prose fiction; writing in one of the most abundantly creative ages of the English novel, he never turned his critical attentions to Dickens, Thackeray, the Brontës, George Eliot, Meredith, or the earlier works of Hardy or James. His letters reveal that in the latter part of his life, at least, he read several of these authors with admiration; but his taste was not formed on them, and he never incorporated any recognition of their achievements into his critical pronouncements. For Arnold, it would seem, poetry still outranked prose, Europe largely outranked England, the past always outranked the present.

Moreover, as with so many critics, his sympathies were most limited with those qualities he least shared. He penned several good lines about Macaulay ('a born rhetorician . . . a perpetual semblance of hitting the right nail on the head without the reality' [iii. 210; v. 317]), but his considered conclusion was 'Macaulay is to me uninteresting, mainly, I think, from a dash of intellectual vulgarity which I find in all his performance' (L ii. 134). The 'intellectual vulgarity' all readers of Macaulay will recognize, but it is surely a limitation of Arnold's own to find him *therefore* 'uninteresting'. The charge of over-fastidiousness has some bite here. Again, his judgement of Charlotte Brontë (admittedly only in an early letter) indicates the limits of his range in another direction. 'Why is *Villette* disagreeable? Because the writer's mind contains nothing but hunger, rebellion, and rage, and therefore that is all she can, in fact, put into her book' (L i. 34). Even if one allowed that there was a grain of truth in this observation (though by the exaggeration of the 'all' it forfeits much respect), it is still a reminder that those who are themselves culturally 'central' can too easily take offence at the tone of such protests and extend too little imaginative sympathy to their sources. And one might extend the list of his defects by including some of the tics I have already mentioned in passing, such as his obsession with 'ranking' authors in the timeless canon, or his increasing tendency to over-value weighty moral utterance.

But despite all this, his most recent biographer is right to declare that Arnold 'is a very great critic: *every* English and American critic since his time has felt his impact'. This is partly because he characterized in unforgettable ways the role that criticism—that kind of literary criticism which is also cultural criticism, and thus, as I shall suggest in the next chapter, a sort of informal political theory—can and must play in modern societies. He introduced a level of self-consciousness about the critic's activities which will never go away. But he also earns the tribute because at his best, as in the last of his Homer lectures or several of the essays in *Essays in Criticism*, he could combine the fine discrimination, the just appraisal, and the telling phrase in a way that has few equals. He could be economical yet devastating: he pounced on F. W. Newman's description of Homer's style as 'quaint, garrulous, prosaic, low': 'Search the English language for a word which does not apply to Homer, and you could not fix on a better than *quaint*, unless perhaps you fixed on one of the other three' (i. 119). He could be mercilessly perceptive: Kinglake's style, he damningly pointed out, was that of 'the good editorial': 'it has glitter without warmth, rapidity without ease, effectiveness without charm. Its characteristic is, that it has no *soul*; all it exists for, is to get its ends, to make its points, to damage its adversaries, to be admired, to triumph' (iii. 255). He could be discerning and exact: 'the emotion of Marcus Aurelius does not quite light up his morality, but it suffuses it; it has not power to melt the clouds of effort and austerity quite away, but it shines through them and glorifies them; it is a spirit, not so much of gladness and elation, as of gentleness and sweetness; a delicate and tender sentiment, which is less than joy and more than resignation' (iii. 149). And he could be shrewdly realistic: Joubert may have had 'less power and richness than his English parallel, [but] he had more tact and penetration. He was more *possible* than Coleridge; his doctrine was more intelligible than Coleridge's, more receivable' (iii. 193). When these elements combine, as they do in Arnold's best work, we get that sense of the irresistible rightness of the judgements that only comes when we are reading one of the great critics.

5 The social critic

When Arnold left for his tour of French schools in March 1859, he was 36 years old. He had established a reputation as a gifted and decidedly intellectual poet; as a result of a couple of strongly classsicizing prefaces and a few lectures as Professor of Poetry at Oxford he had begun to acquire some standing as a critic. But his published work had given little sign of an interest in larger social matters, and, perhaps surprisingly, he had yet to appear as the author of a single periodical article. Yet by the time *Culture and Anarchy* first appeared as a book ten years later, Arnold's name conjured up a particular style and vein of social criticism he had made his own, and with which it has been associated ever since. The apparently apolitical young literary dandy of the 1840s and the austerely classical aesthetic theorist of the 1850s had matured into the formidable social critic with a seldom rivalled capacity to tease, charm, provoke, and irritate his countrymen out of their habitual complacency.

That five-month visit to France was as much the occasion as the catalyst for Arnold to emerge in a new public role. From his private letters, we can see that certain themes had long been maturing in his mind. His Francophilia had, after all, always involved more than a taste for *bons mots* and beautiful actresses: his admiration of French intellectuality, of the 'idea-moved masses' of their democracy, and of the embodiment of these values in a rational, active state were already of long standing in 1859. Moreover, his experience in the dismally provincial society of the Dissenters whose schools he had been inspecting for the last eight years formed the strongest counterpoint to this selectively perceived ideal. The future author of *Culture and Anarchy* was well supplied with preconceptions when he set out for Paris.

Democracy and education

He published his first pamphlet on political matters while still abroad. *England and the Italian Question* was a rather naïvely hopeful attempt to convince the English governing class to take a more sympathetic view of France's intervention in Italy in that year, largely on the improbable grounds that Napoleon III was only acting as the expression of the French people's passion for justice and democratic principles. But woven in with this plea was an adumbration of what was to become a characteristic Arnoldian theme, namely that an hereditary aristocracy, whatever its political achievements in the past, was ill-equipped to understand a modern world that was essentially governed by ideas and inevitably moving towards greater social equality. He expanded this argument in an impressive essay with which he prefaced the published version of his official report on French schools in 1861, and which he subsequently reprinted separately under the title 'Democracy', a title that justly acknowledges the argument's Tocquevillian pedigree.

Characteristically, Arnold focused not upon democracy as a set of political institutions, still less upon the economic arrangements these might presuppose, but upon the question of cultural values and intellectual and aesthetic standards. 'The difficulty for democracy', he wrote in 1861, 'is how to find and keep high ideals' (ii. 17). It was a variant of a problem that preoccupied many nineteenth-century social thinkers: how were increasingly democratic societies to sustain those cultural and political activities that had in the past depended upon the existence of a wealthy and leisured aristocracy? Arnold thought that there were two reasons why the problem assumed a particularly acute form in England. The first was the way in which the sturdy independence which was such a feature of the English national character (Arnold shared his contemporaries' predilection for talking in this vein) had combined with a peculiar political history to produce a very deep antipathy to allowing the state to play a more active part. And secondly, from a rather similar combination of causes, the English middle class, which was thus left to determine the future tone of national life, exhibited a painfully narrow and impoverished conception of what that life might be.

Faced with this diagnosis, Arnold turned in the first instance to education. At that date, there was, in sad contrast to countries like France or Prussia, no national system of education in England.

The state did not take even the first steps towards compulsory elementary education until after 1870; secondary education, such as there was, was left entirely to private enterprise. Arnold deplored this neglect of what he took to be one of the most fundamental tasks of the state in a civilized community. In his provocatively-titled *A French Eton* (1864), an attractively informal and concrete account of some of the French schools he had visited, he lauded the virtues of the *lycée* system. But it was not only the practical superiority of the French arrangements he wished to draw attention to; it was also the example they provided of looking to the state to uphold and promote the highest ideals of civilization.

Indeed, at times Arnold seems less concerned with the merits of a state system of education in its own right, and more with the way it instantiated a more expansive conception of the state as the embodiment of the national life more generally. As he put it in 1861, in the introduction to the published version of his official report:

The question is whether . . . the nation may not now find advantage in voluntarily allowing to [the government] purposes somewhat ampler, and limits somewhat wider within which to execute them, than formerly; whether the nation may not thus acquire in the State an ideal of high reason and right feeling, representing its best self, commanding general respect, and forming a rallying point for the intelligence and for the worthiest instincts of the community, which will herein find a true bond of union. (ii. 19)

The germ of much of the argument of *Culture and Anarchy* is evident here, as is that elevated vocabulary that was to earn Arnold so much hostility then and since. We may find it hard to discern the expression of 'right reason' and 'best selves' in the grubby buildings erected by local School Boards after 1870, but even if Arnold's language still jars, the principles for which he argued were handsomely realized in the legislation which established the extensive state education system of the twentieth century.

On this question of state action, Arnold was self-consciously (at times perhaps a touch too self-consciously) challenging the established pieties of the day. He argued that there was little danger in England of the state exceeding its powers; the safeguards, especially the fierce public antagonism to state action, were too strong for that. Arnold was not indifferent to the dangers an over-mighty state could pose to the liberties of the individual, but he perceived that this case did not want for advocates in mid-nineteenth century England, and concentrated on pressing the claims of the opposite position. This led to a notable difference of view between Arnold and the most obviously comparable social critic among his contemporaries, John Stuart Mill. The question of education crystallized the difference. Mill, fearful of the coercive power of an unchallenged democracy, argued that schools should not actually be run by the state lest that give the state the power to impose its own views and press uniformity upon the next generation (though he accepted the need for the state to set and monitor minimal educational standards); he saw in the variety of different private provision of education the best defence of individuality. Arnold, by contrast, feared that the danger of leaving education in private hands was that it would only be conducted by the narrowest or most eccentric or provincial of criteria. As he put it in 1861:

By giving to schools . . . a public character, the state can bring the instruction in them under a criticism which the stock of knowledge and judgment in our middle class is not at present able to supply. By giving to them a national character, it can confer on them a greatness and a noble spirit which the tone of these classes is not of itself at present able to impart.

In Arnold's mind, the contrast to 'national' or 'public', terms which he always endowed with strong positive connotations, was 'provincial' or 'sectarian'; even in this relatively early essay, the idea that what is 'central' is *in itself* superior to what is marginal or merely local is already evident.

Not long after he wrote these lines, Arnold was faced with a proposed alteration in the relation between state and education in England that was the complete antithesis of his ideals. The grant made by the state to elementary schools of the kind Arnold inspected was minimal, but it both enabled them to escape the worst features of the Dotheboys Hall pattern, and was an expression, however limited, of the nation's interest in the task of civilizing the next generation. In 1861, the government, prompted on this issue by Robert Lowe, an expenditure-cutting Liberal of Utilitarian descent, proposed to reduce this grant very considerably, and to institute instead a system of examinations for all children in these schools to determine whether the basics of the 'three Rs' were being satisfactorily instilled: a payment would then be made to the school for every pupil who satisfied the examiners. (This was known as 'the Revised Code' or system of 'payment by results'.) To Arnold, this seemed an appalling expression of the mean-mindedness which disfigured the English middle class; it would also reduce the schools to cramming, and would involve the abandonment of any aspiration to shape the young more fully. He criticized the scheme in one of his most carefully-argued articles, 'The Twice-Revised Code' (1862), in the course of which he, with some courage, made several stinging observations about Lowe, who was technically his superior ('a political economist of such force, that had he been by when the Lord of the harvest was besought to "send labourers into his harvest", he would certainly have remarked of that petition that it was "a defiance of the laws of supply and demand" [ii. 243]). He concluded his article (which seems not to have provoked the official reprisals he had feared) with a fine rhetorical passage, characteristic of his high polemical style. The supporters of the Revised Code were numerous, including

those extreme Dissenters who for the last ten years have seemed bent on proving how little the future of the country is to owe to their intelligence. There are the friends of economy at any price, always ready to check the hundreds of the national expenditure, while they let the millions go. There are the selfish vulgar of the upper classes, saying in their hearts that this educational philanthropy is all rubbish, and that the less a poor man learns except his handicraft the better. There are the clever and fastidious, too far off from its working to see the substantial benefits which a system, at all national, of popular education confers on the lower classes, but offended by its superficial faults. All these will be gratified by the triumph of the Revised Code, and they are many. And there will be only one sufferer:—*the education of the people.* (ii. 243)

As this last quotation indicates, Arnold was broadening the range of his cultural criticism. Previously, it had been 'spasmodic' poets and leaden-fingered translators of Homer who had felt the lash of his prose; now whole classes—at times, the whole nation—were similarly upbraided. As a result, in the 1860s Arnold was involved in an almost continuous series of overlapping controversies. It was also the decade that saw the composition of his two most enduring works. These two facts were connected, with each at various moments being one of the causes of the other. The seductive style and sheer quality of his social criticism ensured an abundant response, as did its tone of cultivated superiority: it may, after all, be more enraging to be told you are vulgar than to be told you are wicked. But conversely, Arnold thrived on controversy, as he occasionally admitted: it stirred his creativity and aroused him to some of his most imaginative and sustained writing.

With late twentieth-century condescension, we may feel that Victorian society provided Arnold with an altogether too easy target, all earnest humbug and ugly antimacassars. But that was not how it seemed at the time. Arnold was attacking a society that was at the peak of its self-confidence: it was not used to having some of its most cherished beliefs treated with scornful mockery, and still less to having the virtues of other nations held up for emulation. John Bull had shown his superiority over the foreigner at Waterloo, just as he was doing again in every workshop and factory in the land; he could pride himself, and often did, on being heir to a unique tradition of political liberty, sensible religion, and respectable manners. Now, Arnold was not unappreciative of England's fortunate political development, and, as his correspondence reveals, he was responsive to an idea of national greatness: he felt despondent at the prospect of England 'declining into a sort of greater Holland' (L i. 360), and inhabited his own Englishness with ease and some pride, for all that some of his critics charged him with a want of patriotism. But these deep emotional allegiances only made him detest English complacency and parochialism the more, and his diverse essays in social criticism were united by the purpose, much frustrated but resourcefully prosecuted, of teasing, educating, and shaming his countrymen into a greater awareness of these shortcomings.

Among those who did not take kindly to being schooled in this way was that pugnacious Victorian controversialist, James Fitzjames Stephen. He had no patience with what he took to be Arnold's fastidious nose-holding about the unintellectual English in 'The Function of Criticism', and responded with the delicacy of a wounded rhinoceros in an article entitled 'Mr Arnold and his Countrymen'. Indirectly, but not inappropriately, he thereby provoked what was eventually to become, as *Culture and Anarchy*, the classic indictment of English philistinism. Arnold brooded upon a reply to Stephen's attack while spending several months of 1865 on a tour of the higher education arrangements of the Continent, especially Prussia, which sharpened his sense of England's backwardness in these matters. Upon his return he gave vent to his talent for social satire in a series of pieces later collected under the title *Friendship's Garland*, a work of wit and high spirits that should be required reading for all those who think of Arnold only as an uninvitingly heavy moralist.

Arnold took up and refashioned a familiar device of social criticism, the ostensibly innocent observations of a (fictitious) visiting foreigner, here a young Prussian *savant* called Arminius Von Thunder-ten-Tronckh. The name was taken from that eighteenth-century classic of the genre, Voltaire's *Candide*, though the relation to this character of Arnold as 'editor' is more immediately reminiscent of Carlyle's similar relation to 'Herr Teufelsdröckh' in *Sartor Resartus*. Arminius's unflattering observations on the benighted ways of his hosts were conveyed largely through the medium of a series of letters to the *Pall Mall Gazette* by one 'Matthew Arnold' (who gave 'Grub Street' as his address), a persona which enabled Arnold to play further variations on his habitual vein of ironic self-mockery, as when the 'Matthew Arnold' figure reports himself cut by an English acquaintance and left standing, 'with my hat in my hand, practising all the airs and graces I have learnt on the Continent' (v. 75).

Friendship's Garland also contains elements of extravagant burlesque reminiscent of Dickens's social satires. With exaggerated pride, 'Matthew Arnold' introduces Arminius to the very crown of the cherished English system of local self-government, the magistrates' bench, occupied on this occasion by three representative local worthies: Lord Lumpington, a peer of broad acres and narrow prejudices; the Reverend Esau Hittall, whose 'performance of his sacred duties never warms up except when he lights on some passage about hunting and fowling'; and the self-made manufacturer, Bottles Esquire. Arminius inquires after the education of these gentlemen, the extent of their professional training in Roman Law, Jurisprudence, and the like. 'Matthew Arnold' replies archly that the squire and the rector were fortunate enough to have 'followed the grand old, fortifying, classical curriculum' (for all his own devotion to the Ancients, Arnold was well aware of the shortcomings of the grind that in practice passed for a classical education in the Public Schools). '"But did they know anything when they left?" asked Arminius. "I have seen some longs and shorts of Hittall's", said I, "about the Calydonian Boar, which were not bad. . . ."'

However, it is when he turns to the education of Bottles Esquire that the slyly ironic gives way to the exuberantly farcical. The bleak utilitarianism of the world of the commercial classes stirred Arnold's deepest antipathies, and in this case he manages to tar the proponents of a more practical scientific education with the same brush.

'Here we get into another line altogether, but a very good line in its way, too. Mr Bottles was brought up at the Lycurgus House Academy, Peckham. You are not to suppose from the name of Lycurgus that any Latin and Greek was taught in the establishment; the name only indicates the moral discipline, and the strenuous, earnest character, imparted there. As to the instruction, the thoughtful educator who was principal of Lycurgus House Academy—Archimedes Silverpump, Ph.D., you must have heard of him in Germany?—had modern views. "We must be men of our age", he used to say. "Useful knowledge, living languages, and the forming of the mind through observation and experiment, these are the fundamental articles of my educational creed." Or, as I have heard his pupil Bottles put it in his expansive moments after dinner . . . : "Original man, Silverpump! fine mind! fine system! None of your antiquated rubbish—all practical work—latest discoveries in science—mind constantly kept excited—lots of interesting experiments—lights of all colours—fizz! fizz! bang! bang! That's what I call forming a man!"'

Culture and Anarchy

Arnold never wrote a *book* called *Culture and Anarchy* any more than he did one called *Essays in Criticism*. Indeed, the idea of bringing together several of his articles as a book does not appear in his correspondence until May 1868, when most of the constituent pieces had already been published; the title, which now seems so inevitably right, appears only to have been settled on a month or two before its publication in January 1869. The book, as is so often true of works that later have classic status thrust upon them, was not at first a great commercial success; a second edition was not called for until 1875. But in the course of the twentieth century, and perhaps for some very twentieth-century reasons, the book has joined that select library of works of non-fiction which the educated person feels guilty about not having read. Where *Essays in Criticism* could be seen as Arnold's Epistles to the Philistines, this was the Gospel according to St Matthew, a Gospel which several generations of zealous missionaries have since preached to the dark corners of the earth.

The piecemeal composition of the book over a period of more than a year left its mark in various ways, as generations of puzzled readers have cause to testify. For example, one chapter will make reference to published criticisms of the preceding chapter, and the long Preface, which was written last, is clearly addressing a rather different political and religious situation from that supposed by the first few chapters proper. But the periodical origins of the work are also a source of strengths, such as its conversational, at times almost intimate, discursive tone. Arnold's prose more generally has been characterized as a monologue masquerading as a dialogue, but there is a genuinely responsive rhythm to much of his writing in this book: which of the other great English prose writers, after all, could get away with beginning not just a sentence or a paragraph but a *chapter* with the argumentative conjunction 'But'?

The book is linked to *Essays in Criticism* both by the thread of controversy and by the purpose signalled in its subtitle: 'An Essay in Political and Social Criticism'. No section of English society entirely escaped his critical scrutiny, and among the happy coinages for which the work is remembered was his characterization of the three main classes as Barbarians, Philistines, and Populace. (Interestingly, the first and last of these terms are in effect classical allusions, while the middle one is, of course, biblical: these two sources always remained the chief reference-points of Arnold's thought and sensibility.) But although the aristocracy and the working class by no means escaped censure (the former perhaps being let off a little more lightly than the latter), the central target of the book, as of Arnold's work in general, was 'the bad civilisation of the English middle class'. *Culture and Anarchy* is a sustained protest against what he saw as the intellectual, aesthetic, and emotional narrowness of English society—against its puritan moralism, its provincialism, its smugness and complacency, its lack of interest in ideas or feeling for style, its pinched and cramped ideals of human excellence; against, in short, its 'philistinism'.

On the strength of this work, or at least of a strongly pre-conceived and superficial reading of it, Arnold is sometimes re-cruited to the ranks of those retrospectively canonized figures, the Victorian 'critics of industrialism'. Certainly Arnold, like all his sensitive contemporaries, was dismayed at some of the features of the factory system and its attendant squalors, but, unlike some of the best-known of those contemporaries, he did not take these features to be an emblem of the endemic sickness of modern society, and, exceptionally among the great Victorian social critics, he was almost silent about political economy. Arnold was responding not to the novelty of industrialism, but to the older and broader con-ception of 'commercial society', of which his criticism might rather be called cultural than sociological. This characterization of Arnold's concern is confirmed when we consider that, in so far as his work had an explicit historical foundation (which was not in fact very far), he dated the malaise of English life not from the Industrial Revolution of the late eighteenth century, but from the linked religious and commercial developments of the early seventeenth. Like several subsequent English critics, T. S. Eliot and F. R. Leavis among them, he tended to idealize what he took to be the vigorous and expressive life of Elizabethan England, the great creative epoch of English history and literature alike, when English culture was not yet divorced from the mainstream of the European tradition. But then, as he had memorably put it in *Essays in Criticism*, 'the great English middle class, the kernel of the nation, the class whose intelligent sympathy had upheld a Shakespeare, entered the prison of Puritanism and had the key turned on its spirit there for two hundred years' (iii. 121).

The 'prison of Puritanism' is a striking phrase, but like many of Arnold's more resonant categories it is not always clear how far 'Puritanism' here is intended to stand for some ideal-typical set of qualities and how far it is supposed to refer to a particular historical embodiment of those qualities (the question will arise again with his famous pairing of 'Hellenism' and 'Hebraism'). Certainly, in this case he was less concerned with the details of seventeenth-century denominational strife than with the way the severer strains of Protestantism—those sects which had refused to acquiesce in the Anglican Settlement and hence were known as Nonconformists or, more commonly, Dissenters—had coloured, in drab and sombre hues, the texture of English life more generally. Ultimately, the importance Arnold assigned to Puritanism in English history was itself a reflection of his preoccupation with the part played by its descendants in Victorian Britain.

It is, I think, almost impossible to overestimate the importance of Arnold's response to Dissent in shaping his social criticism. Some of those modern readers who, on political grounds, find Arnold's feeling for 'centrality' not to their taste have tended to assume that the divisiveness and conflict which he denounced must have been that between social classes. In fact, it was the temper of religious sectarianism that most disturbed Arnold. As we shall see at greater length in the next chapter, religious issues divided Victorian society more deeply, fiercely, and consistently than any other; the obstructive, oppositional activities and sheer noise-making capacities of the Dissenters were formidable, as several Government ministers could ruefully testify. Arnold, of course, had ample first-hand experience of this sectarian temper from his school-inspecting duties: some of the most stinging sentences in *Culture and Anarchy* may have formed in his mind as he endured the company of stiff-backed Congregational merchants and righteous Baptist farmers while visiting the outlying parts of his territory. As he wrote in a letter in 1869, the year of *Culture and Anarchy*'s publication: 'The feeling of the harm their [the Dissenters'] isolation from the main current of thought and culture does in the nation, a feeling that has been developed in me by going about among them for years, is the source of all that I have written on religious, political and social subjects.'

For many readers coming to *Culture and Anarchy* for the first time, and knowing of its reputation as a classic discussion of large issues about politics and culture, it is disconcerting to find that the long

Preface with which the book opens seems to be almost exclusively about the various disadvantages suffered by Dissenters in not belonging to an Established Church. But although the prominence of this issue in the Preface owed something to the eddying currents of contemporary controversies, Arnold's discussion of it tells us much about the shape of his preoccupations and whole cast of mind. It was not only that the Dissenters, with their strictness of conscience, their puritanism, their narrow biblical literalism, their aesthetic poverty and their cultural provincialism, both largely caused and most powerfully embodied all that Arnold found wrong with the life of the English middle class. It was also, and less obviously, that the very fact of being members of a Dissenting sect was, Arnold argued, a cultural handicap for the Nonconformists themselves.

He was not here referring to any legal or educational disadvantages which the Dissenters had historically suffered from, but which had largely, though not entirely, been removed when he was writing. What he was talking about, and what he characterized quite brilliantly, was the kind of deformation suffered by those who define themselves *primarily* in terms of some sectarian opposition to an established order. What he saw was that those whose fundamental identity was given to them by their status as members of a sect could not help but respond to all ideas and values, and judge all issues, from the constraining vantage-point of the person with a grievance. We are perhaps even more preoccupied than were Arnold's contemporaries with the rights of those who are the victims of various kinds of oppression or deprivation. Arnold was certainly not without sympathy for those who suffered from injustice or unfairness, but he also saw the rather less obvious side of the coin, the way in which the person with a grievance can become the prisoner of that grievance, obsessed with a single issue, consumed by resentment and a sense of exclusion. We see again, as in his notion of criticism discussed in the last chapter, his constant search for correctives to all forms of one-sidedness and obsessiveness.

That the Church of England was the ideal corrective in this case, or even an acceptable one, may seem more doubtful. Arnold's own religious views will be discussed more fully in the next chapter, but his conviction of the *cultural* value of sharing in the traditions and rites of an established church was a central feature of his social criticism. Writing as someone temperamentally antipathetic to both biblical literalism and theological abstractions, Arnold arguably failed to show sufficient sympathy with the views of those for whom these matters were literally more important than life or death; the Dissenter could hardly be responsive to the beautiful cadences of *The Book of Common Prayer* when he believed that its use would entail eternal damnation. But in *Culture and Anarchy*, at least, Arnold was concerned rather with ways of bringing whole sections of the population out of the defensive prickliness of their spiritual isolation and into contact with a larger, more enriching experience, and for this purpose it was perhaps forgivable for Dr Arnold's son to think of the church of Cranmer and the Authorised Version as a civilizing agent.

Of course, the wilful, sectarian temper Arnold was criticizing expressed itself in political as well as religious terms. It issued in the doctrine that Arnold pilloried as 'Doing As One Likes'. This represented that central strain in Victorian political attitudes (powerfully expressed in, but not confined to, the Liberal party) which insisted on the right of the individual to go about his business without let or hindrance from his fellow-citizens or from the state. Clearly, this could issue in a policy of extreme *laissez-faire* in social and economic matters, and this is the aspect of Victorian Liberalism that has most engaged the attention of later historians. But Arnold was, as ever, concerned less with particular policies than with the deeper attitudes they expressed. In this exaggerated individualism he detected both a low aspiration, in being content with one's existing wants, and a kind of hubris in assuming that the isolated individual can adequately determine his pattern of life for himself. The ethos of popular Liberalism—on the one hand jealous of its rights and touchy about being patronized, on the other proud of its material achievements and dismissive of cultivation and refinement—had no room for 'high ideals' or notions of a 'best self', and hence was incapable of rising to 'the notion, so familiar on the Continent and to antiquity, of the *State*—the nation in its collective and corporate character' (v. 117). *Culture and Anarchy* was a bravura attempt to domesticate these alien notions and

81

to make such elevated language part of the common currency of English thought.

Arnold had the shrewd controversialist's eye for ways of gaining attention for his ideas, and a talent for condensing an argument into a catch-phrase. He was delighted to find that his amusing labels for the three great classes of English society caught on almost immediately ('I think *barbarian* will stick', he informed his mother in 1868 [L i. 450]), but these were if anything overshadowed by a yet more lasting coinage, which again owed its origin to Heine, the binary categories of 'Hebraism' and 'Hellenism'. These terms characterize the two great traditions of thought and feeling that had influenced the Western world, but also stand for the two tendencies which are constantly struggling for dominance within each individual. His various definitions of these two terms prove, as always in Arnold, to be diverse and not always obviously compatible, but the outlines are clear enough. 'The governing idea of Hellenism', as he puts it most pithily, 'is *spontaneity of consciousness*; that of Hebraism, *strictness of conscience*' (v. 165). Hebraism, that is, fixes above all on the idea of duty, of moral rules, of the subjugation of the self: its chief concern is to act rightly, and the emphasis here falls not only on the 'rightly', but also on the 'acting', for Hebraism is an ethic which stresses the exercise of will. Hellenism, by contrast, concerns itself more with knowledge and beauty, with the play of ideas and the charm of form. Hebraism attacks wrongdoing, moral laxness, and weakness of will; Hellenism attacks ignorance, ugliness, and rigidity of mind. Arnold constantly asserts that society needs a balance between these two forces, since both are essential to the full development of the human spirit, but that it must genuinely be a balance. It will already be obvious that, in his view, Victorian England was far too dominated by the ethic of Hebraism, and his work may be seen as a series of attempts to bring some of the resources of the tradition of Hellenism to bear upon the cramped consciousness of his contemporaries. Actually, although Arnold's explicit and, as it were, official view is that both forces are equally necessary, the attentive reader of *Culture and Anarchy* cannot help but notice that Arnold's characterizations of Hellenism are far more enthusiastic and favourable than those of Hebraism. In part, of course, this is just because it is Hellenism which he believes to be in short supply among his audience, and he needs to obtain a hearing for its virtues and to get its contribution better appreciated. None the less, his prose betrays a limited sympathy for that Augustinian or Calvinist tendency to repress or root out the rebellious urges in the name of obedience and suppression of self that he finds at the root of Hebraism, whereas the passages in which he tries to express the essence of Hellenism have a constant tendency to become lyrical, as in the following example:

> To get rid of one's ignorance, to see things as they are, and by seeing them as they are to see them in their beauty, is the simple and attractive ideal which Hellenism holds out before human nature; and from the simplicity and charm of this ideal, Hellenism, and human life in the hands of Hellenism, is invested with a kind of aerial ease, clearness and radiancy; they are kept full of what we call sweetness and light. (v. 167)

Arnold's adjectives in this passage all evoke, perhaps a little over-insistently, visions of lightness, clearness, brilliance, simplicity; it is the sort of language the guide-books use when they want to describe the impression made by a Greek temple in Mediterranean sunlight, and it can, of course, have the same unfortunate effect on the counter-suggestible reader. But these invocations of the clean lines and serene forms of Greek art may have stirred more powerful resonances among Arnold's classically-educated audience, and certainly they express a deep affinity of his own temperament.

The characterization of Hellenism just quoted also includes another famous Arnoldian phrase, 'sweetness and light'. This became one of those tags that he played with over and over again, a kind of code for what he wanted to identify as the peculiar deficiency of 'the bad civilisation of the English middle class'. It is unfortunate, I think, that the words 'sweetness and light' now have a somewhat unctuous, almost genteel, even anaemic air about them; they suggest too much the mild uplift dispensed by that kind of wet do-gooder who never seems to have felt the pull of any real human appetites. But these were not the connotations Arnold had in mind: indeed, he appropriated the terms (from Swift's fable of the bee and the spider in *The Battle of the Books*) to make a contrast with some of these qualities—he wanted them to stand for gaiety rather than solemnity, for knowledge rather than righteousness, for pure, useless self-exploration rather than corrective, functional, self-improvement. In Arnold's later writings, this strain tends to get overshadowed, even at times displaced, by a more sombre set of preoccupations as he dwells on the need for that 'something not ourselves that makes for righteousness' and for that 'high seriousness' that he looked for in great literature. But in the 1860s he still handled these issues with a lighter touch, and the author of *Culture and Anarchy* manifestly preferred to loll on Parnassus than to crawl up Calvary. Hebraism is, after all, hardly the natural home of the dandy, even the reformed dandy turned cultural critic.

Arnold's Hellenism is not without its problems, however. The Greeks are the unacknowledged heroes of *Culture and Anarchy*, and Arnold has been reproached more than once for adopting a 'Greeker than thou' tone. Although much of his perception of the Greeks was widely shared among their nineteenth-century European admirers—and his work played a significant role in turning these perceptions into the commonplaces of English literary criticism—it is worth remarking how selective, even tendentious, his account was. The language he uses to characterize and celebrate their never-to-be-repeated achievements constantly dwells upon their balance, control, serenity. His famous praise for Sophocles, we recall, was for his ability to 'see life steadily and see it whole', and he endlessly returns to this emphasis on steadiness and balance rather than any unbalancing extremes of passion, displaying always his familiar bias towards unity and wholeness rather than towards any more selective, one-sidedly penetrating and creative play of energy. 'The bent of Hellenism is to follow, with flexible activity, the whole play of the universal order, to be apprehensive of missing any part of it, of sacrificing one part to another' (v. 165).

As an interpretation of the essential qualities of Greek art and thought this could be, and has been, challenged. To contrast with what Arnold calls 'the Greek quarrel with the body and its desires', it would not be too difficult to assemble a different picture that placed their pagan sensuousness in the foreground, or even to focus upon what Nietzsche was soon to call their 'Dionysiac' qualities. Similarly, one could give an account of the great Greek tragedians which emphasized much more their bleak perception of the savage arbitrariness of life rather than a calm vision of seeing it steadily and seeing it whole. The truth surely is that this characterization expresses a deep yearning of *Arnold's* towards these qualities, at least as much as it provides an objective appraisal of the Greeks. It is he, rather than Sophocles or Thucydides, who is 'apprehensive' of getting things out of proportion.

The term, to come to it finally, which stands for the animating idea of the book, the term with which Arnold's name is now indissolubly linked, is, of course, 'culture'. In one of his many phrases which have subsequently become part of our common language, Arnold said that by culture he meant 'the best that has been thought and said'. In implicitly assigning priority to the literary and philosophical over the visual and musical, the phrase faithfully represents Arnold's own cultural tastes, yet in other ways it expresses rather poorly the richness of the idea behind his use of 'culture'. For he treats culture not just as something that we can acquire or possess, but as something that is an active force in its own right. One indication of this is the frequency with which he uses the word with an active verb: culture '*endeavours* to see and learn, and to *make* what it sees and learns prevail', culture '*conceives* of perfection . . . as a harmonious expansion of all the powers which make the beauty and worth of human nature', 'culture has a rough *task to achieve* in this country', and so on.

This simple stylistic fact alone should suggest that he is not talking about some passive body of art and learning whose natural home is the museum and the library, nor simply a set of high-status social activities encased in an aura of snobbery and pretentiousness. He is talking, rather, about an ideal of human life, a standard of excellence and fullness for the development of our capacities, aesthetic, intellectual, and moral. The ideal which culture holds up before us is that of 'perfection' or the 'harmonious expansion of *all* the powers which make the beauty and worth of human nature' (v. 94). Of course, the assumption that *all* our capacities could even in principle be compatible with each other is itself doubtful, unless, with a hint of circularity, there is an implicit restriction to our 'positive' capacities. In his other works, Arnold, like several other prominent Victorian moralists, oscillated a little unsteadily between, on the one hand, affirming the possibility of a harmonious development of *all* our impulses, and, on the other, endorsing the view that the self was a battleground where the forces of the higher self of conscience and rationality were perpetually in conflict with those of the lower self of appetite and animality. I have already suggested how, in some of his later writings, which were the work of a more sombre Arnold, sobered by bereavement and prolonged meditation on religion, he most often inclines to the latter view. But in *Culture and Anarchy*, it is the former view which predominates, partly because he defines perfection as 'the growth and pre-dominance of our humanity proper, as distinguished from our animality' (v. 94), but also perhaps because he is, so to speak, rhetorically on the attack, trying to raise both the tone and the stakes rather than to lower them.

He recognized, of course, that even in this active sense culture is not innate: it is something a true understanding of which is only acquired by effort and by exposure to the results of the efforts of previous generations. But it is certainly something that is, in his view, within reach of everybody, given the right opportunites, not something confined to a small class. 'The great men of culture', as he put it in an important passage,

are those who have had a passion for diffusing, for making prevail, for carrying from one end of society to the other, the best knowledge, the best ideas of their time; who have laboured to divest knowledge of all that was harsh, uncouth, difficult, abstract, professional, exclusive; to humanise it, to make it efficient outside the clique of the cultivated and the learned, yet still remaining the best knowledge and thought of the time, and a true source, therefore, of sweetness and light. (v. 113)

This passage also suggests some of the deeper connections be-tween his notion of culture and the ideal of criticism he had ex-plored in his earlier works. In making 'the best thought of their time' available to a wider audience, what is it that the great men of culture have had to divest it of? The list of adjectives is very striking, and at first sight somewhat heterogeneous: they have divested it of 'all that was harsh, uncouth, difficult, abstract, pro-fessional, exclusive'. Now, 'harsh' and 'difficult' are the sort of adjectives we might expect in such a sentence; the best thought may need to be made a little more accessible and attractive. Similarly,

perhaps, 'abstract' is not an altogether surprising term here: Arnold means not only abstract in form, as the work of many of the
great philosophers may be, but also abstract in the sense of too
removed from the realities of life, too much concerned with the
intellectual values of system and coherence at the expense of recognizing the disorderly actuality of the world. 'Uncouth' is a bit
more surprising, suggestive at first of social rather than intellectual
defects, but I think in the context it is clear that it means something
more like 'badly expressed', 'jargon-ridden', 'too internal to the
preoccupations and language of one individual or group'. These
are in fact all ways of being inaccessible, of being something which
only the insider can understand; much writing by academics may
in this sense rightly be called uncouth. It is at first sight more
surprising to find a term like 'professional' in this list, since we may
have come to think of it as an entirely positive quality. But by
placing it in such company Arnold precisely draws attention to the
sense in which it represents a very questionable value. What links
all these terms is the idea that knowledge, the best thought of the
time, the best that has been thought and said, should not be
imprisoned in a form of expression that is specialized, technical,
idiosyncratic, or private, but should rather be accessible, shareable,
public—part, as we have since come to say, of a common culture.

Analysing his idea of culture in this way also makes clear just
how it could be expected to provide what, on Arnold's diagnosis,
Victorian England most lacked. In contrast to the cramped and
limited models of human excellence provided by the traditions of
provincial, Dissenting England, culture would make available a
larger, richer sense of human possibilities. In contrast to the parochial, second-rate kinds of art and literature favoured by current
middle-class taste, culture would hold up the standard offered by
the very greatest achievements of the human spirit in its long
history. In contrast to the divisive, sectarian, tiresomely controversial spirit fostered within the confines of individual religious
denominations, political parties, or social classes, culture would act
as a unifying force, replacing the parochial with the universal, the
sectarian with the national, the exclusive with the inclusive. This
idea of the capacity of culture to unify and heal the divisions in

society has been (as we shall see in Chapter 7) one of Arnold's most potent legacies.

'*A Liberal of the Future*'

The question of where the author of *Culture and Anarchy* should be placed in the political spectrum as conventionally understood puzzled some of its first readers, and has continued to vex commentators ever since. The fact that his most vehement critics at the time would all have described themselves as Liberals, and that the work was praised by the Tory leader Disraeli, does not by itself establish the book's conservative identity, though it indicates why the question insists on being asked. Arnold, of course, had already laid it down that criticism remained true to itself by 'keeping aloof from what is called "the practical view of things"', but in practice he was certainly not above using his lofty vantage-point to broadcast judgements on several of the great issues of the day, especially in the last decade of his life when he was a well-known public figure whose utterances were eagerly solicited by the editors of the leading reviews. The political writings of Arnold's last years share the defects of his late literary essays: they can be formulaic and repetitive, indulging a propensity for sententious windiness that the easy availability of recognized pulpits always seems to encourage. But they can also be trenchant and outspoken, and reading them should certainly dispel any lazy notion that Arnold's elevated notion of the state entailed an uncritical endorsement of the conventional wisdom of the governing class of his day.

The difficulty of encompassing Arnold's political thought with any of the conventional labels is acutely illustrated by the juxtaposition of his important essay on 'Equality' (1878) with his later writings on Ireland. 'Equality' expressed a view that was deliberately heterodox and remarkably radical (the more so for the fact that it was first given as an address to the gathering of scientists, literati, and members of high society who made up the audience at the Royal Institution). It consisted of a sustained denunciation of the extreme inequality of the distribution of property in Britain, and of the impress which that had left on social relations. 'Our inequality materialises our upper class, vulgarises our middle class, brutalises our lower' (viii. 302). He particularly deplored the way in which the laws of bequest and inheritance permitted and even encouraged this excessive concentration of property in a few hands, and, as so often, he made his point by means of a running contrast with France where the law reinforced tradition to prevent such concentration, and where social life was consequently much freer and less deferential. In this essay, Arnold was willing to be entirely pragmatic about what system of property-holding it may be in society's interests to endorse, a view which it is perhaps surprising but certainly creditable to find a hard-pressed man of letters extending, in a companion piece on 'Copyright' (1880), to intellectual property as well. (More predictably, this latter article argued for those two perennial wants of the book-writing class, lower prices and better legal protection against pirated foreign editions.)

Ireland taxed the judgement and tolerance of all English politicians and political thinkers in the late nineteenth century, and brought out a revealing mixture of responses in Arnold. He was sympathetic to Irish grievances and critical of the twin pillars of the Protestant Ascendancy, the Irish (i.e. Anglican) church and the English landowners. He particularly attempted to modify English prejudice against Catholicism (a religion whose aesthetic richness and close ties to the European cultural tradition he anyway found more appealing than most forms of Protestantism), and at times one cannot help feeling that his sympathy for the Irish cottier comes as much from a sense that he is a fellow-victim of English puritan bigotry as from any closer understanding of his economic hardships. At the same time, the Arnold who regarded 'anarchy' as the worst of all political conditions, and who upheld the doctrine of 'force till right be ready', condoned the fierce enforcement of the law in Ireland, including the suspension of civil liberties, when faced with the organized campaign of disruption in the 1880s, and he was an unyielding opponent of Gladstone's scheme for Home Rule. Like many mid-century liberal intellectuals, he was in his last years profoundly alienated from what he perceived as Gladstone's demagogic brand of Liberalism.

Since so much of Arnold's writing was a kind of prolonged family quarrel with the English middle class, he was bound to have intimate but complex relations with that class's chief political expression, the Liberal Party. His many descriptions of himself as a Liberal invariably arrive towing some qualifying phrase behind them—such as 'a Liberal tempered by experience', or, in a phrase he particularly favoured, 'a Liberal of the Future' (e.g. ix. 138). Some of his critics might have preferred to rephrase this in the formula of 'Lord give me Liberalism, but not yet', so fastidiously dissatisfied was he with most incarnations of Liberalism in the present. But he saw it as his role to stand back from the fray and tell the Liberals some unpalatable truths about the narrowness of their views, and conservatives are always ready to seize with delight upon those who presume to criticize radical orthodoxies. But Arnold was no friend to Toryism. The Liberals 'at best . . . are in a very crude state', he wrote to his sister (not altogether tactfully, since she was married to one of their leaders), 'and with little light or help in them at present. But through their failing, and succeeding, and gradual improvement lies our way, our only way; I have no doubt of that.' (ix. 370)

Certainly, some of the presiding spirits who did most to influence his social thought make, when taken together, what might seem to be an odd pedigree for a Liberal: Burke, Newman, Carlyle, to name the most obvious. Actually, he had never been entirely comfortable with the blacker side of Carlyle's reactionary politics, and explicitly repudiated his increasingly unconfined authoritarianism. Similarly, for all his reverence for John Henry Newman, both personally and as the embodiment of the spirit of his beloved Oxford, Arnold was undeniably and unshakeably a liberal in the intellectual and religious senses which Newman had spent his life denouncing, and implicitly he ranged himself on the side of Goethe and Heine and all those whom he described (borrowing yet another phrase of Heine's) as 'soldiers in the Liberation War of humanity' (iii. 107) for their attempts to carry through the best features of the programme of the Enlightenment.

His relation to Burke is more teasing. He fully shared the deep admiration that was so common in nineteenth-century England, calling him 'our greatest political thinker' (ix. 287), quoting him often, and, suggestively, taking from him the epigraph to both *Essays in Criticism* and *The Popular Education of France*. But as these and the other contexts in which he cites him make clear, Arnold valued Burke as a writer and as one who 'treats politics with . . . thought and imagination', and not, as he has increasingly been treated in the twentieth century, as the chief source for conservative political theory. Arnold noticeably preferred Burke writing about Ireland or America, where he displayed a magnanimity and balance Arnold could identify with, to Burke writing about France, where both Arnold's general Francophilia and his specific enthusiasm for 1789 were sorely taxed ('there is much in his view of France and her destinies which is narrow and erroneous' [L i. 250]). No writer who believed, as Arnold did, that the French Revolution was 'the greatest, the most animating event in history' could be regarded as an unproblematic disciple of Burke, still less could he be anything but an extremely awkward recruit to the ranks of conservatism.

As Arnold himself rightly observed, the notion of the state that he was struggling to introduce into English life was 'familiar to Antiquity and on the Continent'. It has been well said of Arnold that he had a strong, almost Roman, sense of the state, but little feel for the people: in this sense, he was a republican but not a democrat (the influence of his father, the historian of the Roman Republic, was strong here). Even more marked were his affinities with that Idealist tradition of political thought that stretches back from, most notably, Hegel and Rousseau to Aristotle and, above all, Plato. Though he found systematic philosophy uncongenial, Arnold was temperamentally something of a Platonist, with all the Platonist's vulnerability to being dazzled by the beauty of his own ideals to the neglect of their abuse in practice. This surely helps to explain why Arnold has attracted charges of authoritarianism. But this deep intellectual affinity also suggests what might be described as the 'anti-political' character of his thought.

This is well caught in a passage in *Culture and Anarchy* where he is talking about what is involved in coming to recognize ourselves as members of a state in his elevated sense. We come, he wrote (here very much the residuary legatee of Broad Church historiography and hence, indirectly, of German Idealism), 'to make the state more and more the expression, as we say, of our best self, which is not manifold, and vulgar, and unstable and contentious

91

and ever-varying, but one, and noble, and secure, and peaceful, and the same for all mankind' (v. 224). The five negatives in the first part of this sentence all suggest something similar, and their juxtaposition here expresses a deep aversion of Arnold's—an aversion to conflict, cantankerousness, disorder; or, in a word, to anarchy. Arnold's own temperamental affinity for the opposite of these characteristics is evident in the five positive terms in the latter part of the passage, which are all suggestive of rest and order, and, once more, of his deep feeling for centrality and unity.

This helps us to draw several features of his work together. We are reminded of the neoclassical aesthetic of his literary criticism, with its professed desire, not always realized, to get beyond any personal qualities or idiosyncracies of the critic—or even, in a sense, of the writer—in order to display what is permanent and universal. Similarly, one can see his conception of the state as in some ways the political equivalent of 'the grand style'. It is also another facet of that classicism that leads him to overvalue balance, achieved form, and the perfect proportions of the finished object, and to undervalue the untidy but possibly creative experience of searching and struggling. No one with such a strong aversion to conflict as Arnold came to manifest could be an altogether satisfactory writer on politics, but the fact remains that his deep feeling for order and wholeness, and still more his acuity in discerning the emotional and psychological roots of political attitudes, did enable him to characterize the contentious public life of his time with a sharpness and stylishness which have set something of a standard for social critics ever since.

6 The religious critic

The passions of the Victorian reading public could be stirred by religion as by no other subject. Our own more secular age can easily underestimate the force and pervasiveness of nineteenth-century religion and religiosity: it was a society in which a new work of Biblical exegesis could be a best-seller, and where volumes of sermons and theological tracts far outsold novels and other genres. Many of the great intellectual controversies of the century were either directly about religion, or else were given an extra dimension of intensity by their bearing on religious belief: the debate over Darwin's theory of evolution by natural selection is the most obvious example, but the point can be illustrated by episodes in which the Arnold family was more directly involved, from the Tractarian storms of the 1830s, through the scandal of Bishop Colenso's study of the Pentateuch in the 1860s, to the immense vogue of *Robert Elsmere* (a novel by Arnold's niece, Mrs Humphry Ward, about loss of faith) in the 1880s. Furthermore, many of the major political issues of the period revolved around the endorsement and enforcement of religious beliefs and practices: from the skirmishes over Catholic Emancipation in the 1820s to the protracted haggling over the question of allowing an avowed atheist to take his seat in Parliament in the 1880s, Arnold's lifetime was punctuated by political crises about what it meant to be an officially Christian, indeed Anglican, state.

As we have already seen, Arnold had risked the displeasure of large elements of this Christian audience in his literary and social criticism of the 1860s. Indeed, some of his literary judgements seemed like deliberate provocations to the pious, as, for example, in taking a pagan like Marcus Aurelius as a model of spirituality, while his campaign against the narrowness of the Dissenters, culminating in the polemical Preface to *Culture and Anarchy*, had antagonized the most vociferous religious body in the land. But in the 1870s Arnold went further still. He challenged what most of his contemporaries took to be the central doctrinal tenets of Christianity, and he treated the Bible as a literary text like any other. What is intriguing—and what to some readers at the time and since has seemed baffling and perhaps not entirely credible—is that he followed this path in the hope of rescuing Christianity from the abyss of unbelief, and of securing for the Bible its proper place as the pre-eminent sacred book.

The result was that his religious criticism of the 1870s was at once his most popular and his most unpopular writing. Only when he moved on to directly religious topics did he enjoy immediate and significant commercial success as an author. *St Paul and Protestantism* (1870) was the first of his works to go through more than one edition in the year of publication, while *Literature and Dogma* (1873) sold more than any of his writings in his lifetime: by the early twentieth century, sales of this book (including the shortened popular editions Arnold brought out, and the large number of pirated reprints in the United States) probably exceeded 100,000. At the same time, Arnold became the target of sustained criticism and denunciation by representatives of almost every denomination of Christian: several readers, including one bishop, cancelled their subscription to the periodical in which his articles first appeared, and even in the 1880s Arnold recognized that he could not be considered for a certain public appointment because the outcry from the Dissenters would be too strong. Yet he genuinely believed that he was helping to strengthen rather than weaken the position of the Church, and his mother may not have been so wide of the mark, all allowance being made for her fond wish that the son of Dr Arnold should not stray too far from the fold, when she insisted that 'Matt is a good Christian at bottom'.

Whether, or in what sense, Arnold should be described as a Christian does not now seem a very profitable question (on most orthodox definitions he certainly wasn't, on some more Modernist definitions perhaps he was). In so far as Arnold had any identifiable cosmological or metaphysical ideas—which wasn't in fact all that far—he was some kind of Spinozist, finding very congenial Spinoza's mixture of devotion to virtue and vaguely pantheist belief in a natural order in the universe, 'the stream of tendency', in a phrase Arnold was fond of repeating, 'by which all things seek to fulfil the law of their being' (e.g. vi. 10). But he recognized that this kind of rarefied intellectual creed was only likely to speak to a small minority, and his writings on religion are largely concerned with the majority whose chief need he identified as being for a source of that 'joyful and bounding emotion' (iii. 134) which would enable them to respond to the demands of morality.

In general, it now seems that it was where he turned to address eternal questions that he has dated most. Yet his writings on religion reveal the continuity of his preoccupations, as well as the qualities and limits of his mind. In this work we see again his constant concern for the spirit in which a belief is held rather than for the letter of dogma, his abiding sense of the narrow limits of intellection, and his emphasis on experience, judgement, and sensitivity rather than theory, doctrine, or literalism. His writings about the Church of England display in another form his desire for inclusiveness and unity, and his antipathy to sectarianism and partisanship. But we also find, perhaps, some insensitivity to the feelings of exclusion among those less central than himself, as well as a culpable lack of rigour with questions that are unavoidably abstract, and traces of an increasingly exigent moralism that constrained the 'flexibility' that he had urged and embodied in his earlier work.

St Paul and Protestantism

In some ways, the long Preface to *Culture and Anarchy*, which was written at the end of 1868, should be considered as the first of Arnold's religious criticisms, since, as we have seen, it was a sustained coloratura on the disadvantages, both to the Dissenters themselves and to the rest of the nation, arising from the continued separation of the Nonconformists from the Church of England. *St Paul and Protestantism* (1870) was a natural extension of the argument of that Preface. It is a work which can best be characterized as an attempt to outflank the Dissenters intellectually.

The bedrock of their position was that they refused to join the national church because it did not teach the true Gospel; they were the Children of the Word, and they took their stand on their text. But what, asked Arnold suavely, if they have misinterpreted their text? What if the very points of doctrine on which they ground their continued separation prove to be misreadings? The extremer varieties of Protestant made the doctrines of predestination and salvation by faith central, and they claimed the authority of St Paul for so doing. But, argued Arnold, they have made the mistake of turning what was the eloquent expression of emotion in Paul into the elaborate intellectual construction of doctrine. 'What in St Paul is figure and belongs to the sphere of feeling, Puritanism has transported into the sphere of intellect and made thesis and formula' (vi. 8). The whole Calvinist position arises out of inadequately sensitive literary criticism: the mistake has been made by those 'who have not enough tact for style to comprehend his mode of expression' (vi. 22). This has led them further to overlook the fact that Paul was not primarily concerned with such abstract questions as the niceties of different doctrines of salvation, but with 'righteousness'; here we encounter the first of Arnold's many redefinitions of religion when he somewhat tendentiously declares 'Religion is that which binds and holds us to the practice of righteousness' (vi. 33). Calvinism has reared an ingenious system of reasoning, but reasoning is not the essence of religion: St Paul's teachings need to be 'disengaged from the elaborate misconceptions with which Protestantism has overlaid them' (vi. 5).

But the Puritans were not only poor literary critics: they were also stiff-necked and self-important in matters of practice. Here, Arnold revised the dominant Whig historiography, which tended to see the Puritans in the late sixteenth and early seventeenth centuries as the victims of persecution, in the face of which the more general rights of free speech and religious toleration had slowly been won. Arnold emphasises rather the way in which it was the Church of England which in the seventeenth century was the more pluralist and open to development and flexibility in theological matters, and the Puritans who had been rigid and uncompromising. Moreover, the Puritans had repeated their mistake of regarding points of 'opinion' as crucial, whereas Arnold again insisted that the Church 'exists not for the sake of opinion but for the sake of moral practice' (vi. 97), thereby tilting the scales of the argument against the Dissenters from the start. The Puritans had stood out, as their latter-day descendants continued to do, on points of doctrine concerning church organization, which, Arnold insists, is only a secondary issue, not a primary one.

Throughout, his emphasis is on the attitude or cast of mind expressed in and encouraged by the Dissenters' antagonistic relation to the Establishment. Indeed, even when discussing freethinkers it is this rather than the *content* of their beliefs that he concentrates on, as where he says: 'For instance, what in Mr Mill is but a yielding to a spirit of irritable injustice, goes on and worsens in some of his disciples till it becomes a sort of mere blatancy and truculent hardness in certain of them' (vi. 126). Arnold's fine ear for the nuances of emotional tone and psychological attitude caught the character of much nineteenth-century secularism very well here, and in another telling passage he uncovered the psychological dynamic at the root of much sectarianism, religious and political. What is it, he asks, that

the everyday, middle-class Philistine . . . finds so attractive in Dissent? Is it not, as to discipline, that his self-importance is fomented by the fuss, bustle and partisanship of a private sect, instead of being lost in the greatness of a public body? As to worship, is it not that his taste is pleased by usages and words that come down to *him*, instead of drawing him up to *them*; by services which reflect, instead of the culture of great men of religious genius, the crude culture of himself and his fellows? And as to doctrine, is it not that his mind is pleased at hearing no opinion but its own, by having all disputed points taken for granted in its own favour, by being urged to no return upon itself, no development? (vi. 122)

Literature and Dogma

Hardly surprisingly, *St Paul and Protestantism* won Arnold few friends among the Nonconformists, but hasty readers within the Establishment could take comfort and delight from it. However, before long many of them were also to be calling for his blood. St Paul's Epistles were not, after all, the only text which the literary critic might find the theologians had misinterpreted. Moreover, Arnold was broadening the scope of his religious criticism on other counts, too. Where he had previously been disturbed primarily about the consequences of the Dissenters' exclusion from the national church, he now turned to the problem of the threat posed to all forms of Christianity by the increase of unbelief. This was, of course, a topic that much agitated Victorian intellectuals, and there was a particular fear that the working class was growing increasingly indifferent to religion. But in Arnold's view it was orthodox theology that was at fault here. It tied Christianity to the literal truth of the Bible; as it became less and less possible, in the face of both modern science and modern historical scholarship, to adhere to the Bible as a guide in matters of fact, so belief in Christianity would decline, and the influence of the Bible would be lost. Arnold always accepted that it was useless quixotically to throw oneself across the path of the *Zeitgeist*: it was impossible now for the reasonable person to be a Biblical literalist. But perhaps such a reading of the Bible had been, as he put it, 'an immense literary misapprehension' (vi. 276) in the first place. *Literature and Dogma* was the critic's attempt to repair the damage before it was too late. There is a case for saying it is his most extended single work of literary criticism; certainly no single text engaged his critical energies to anything like the same extent as did the Bible.

As part of his criticism of Hebraism in *Culture and Anarchy*, Arnold had already taken his stand by the maxim 'no man, who knows nothing else, knows even his Bible' (v. 184), and in this respect the later book is an extended demonstration of what culture can do.

To understand that the language of the Bible is fluid, passing, and literary, not rigid, fixed, and scientific, is the first step towards a right understanding of the Bible. But to take this very first step, some experience of how men have thought and expressed themselves, and some flexibility of spirit, are necessary; and this is culture. (vi. 152)

But it is not only the literalist who may misjudge the meaning of the Bible: those scholars who commanded nothing but erudition (his readers hardly needed to be told that this was aimed at the Germans, but he told them anyway) also lacked the necessary 'justness of perception', that 'power to estimate the proportion and relation in what we read' (vi. 153, 158). Here, as elsewhere, Arnold was disparaging about the squint-eyed vision of the specialist.

A sophisticated grasp of the place of metaphor and symbol in religious language is one of the great strengths of *Literature and Dogma*. Eschewing theology, it repeatedly falls back on 'experience', though in a spirit far removed from that of reductive empiricism. In its dealings with religious belief it talks more of 'feeling' than of 'thinking'. On point after point, Arnold demonstrates the yield from adopting a more imaginative, comparative reading of the Biblical texts, most consequentially in dealing with the very conception of 'God'. In his view, the Jews 'began with experience', and used metaphor and symbol to translate this experience into poetry; it was later theologians who then sophisticated this into an elaborate theory, purporting to have the standing of a scientific explanation, of an omnipotent God. The 'tact' of the critic was, therefore, now required to re-capture the meaning of the original forms of expression, and what this revealed, as he put it in a forceful passage, was that

the word 'God' is used in most cases as by no means a term of science or exact knowledge, but a term of poetry and eloquence, a term *thrown out*, so to speak, at a not fully grasped object of the speaker's consciousness, a *literary* term, in short; and mankind mean different things by it as their consciousness differs. (vi. 171)

What, notoriously, he concluded to have been the essence of the experience which the Old Testament authors had sought to capture with their use of the term 'God' was 'a consciousness of the not ourselves that makes for righteousness' (vi. 196). Many readers at the time and since have felt that this formula strips the traditional notion of God of all that is wonderful and compelling. Certainly, as a way of 'lighting up morality' there might seem doubtful advantage in replacing the bearded patriarch of popular imagination with the impersonal reach of the long arm of the Law.

His treatment of the New Testament has particularly won admiration from later commentators. One of his most radical contributions here was his insight that 'Jesus was over the heads of his reporters' (e.g. vi. 260). The Jews constantly denatured Jesus's novel teachings by assimilating them to their established categories and expectations, yet despite this, the force of Jesus's message had left its mark in the Gospel record. Jesus brought an inwardness to what had been the sternly legalistic public code of Jewish morality; his characteristic tone Arnold aptly characterized as 'sweet reasonableness'. In all this it is noticeable how Arnold responded with particularly keen appreciation to the poet who wrote the Fourth Gospel, partly, perhaps, because the soaring style of his mysticism confounded the literalists at every turn.

Reading *Literature and Dogma* alongside Arnold's earlier works, one sees that just as he called upon criticism to deliver the truth of the Bible from the clutches of the literalists and the pedants, so in return he exploited its success in this task to make a point in his larger campaign on behalf of criticism's cultural role. The Bible yields its full riches only if read 'with the tact which letters, surely, alone can give', and he was not loath to press the point.

For the thing turns upon understanding the manner in which men have thought, their way of using words, and what they mean by them. And by knowing letters, by becoming conversant with the best that has been thought and said in the world, we become acquainted not only with the history, but also with the scope and powers of the instruments which men employ in thinking and speaking. (vi. 196)

Once again we are reminded that Arnold was not talking about 'literary criticism' in any narrow modern sense.

Indeed, much of the book is taken up with a selective intellectual history of the Western Church, showing how successive generations imposed their own constructions on the literary creations of the ancient Jewish authors. Popular Christianity, especially, became weighed down with this *Aberglaube*, the accretion of supernatural and superstitious beliefs that had grown up around the simplicity of the original message, a message that spoke above all of 'righteousness'. Arnold was insistent that 'the antithesis between *ethical* and *religious* is thus quite a false one', and this led him to his famous definition of religion as 'morality touched by emotion' (vi. 176). This high-sounding tag (Arnold's talent, or weakness, for condensing an argument into a formula never deserted him) has come in for severe criticism, most damningly (originally by F. H. Bradley) for being a tautology. The charge is that Arnold could not have meant touched by just *any* emotion (which he surely did not), but, rather, touched by *religious* emotion, and therefore the definition is circular. The case may not be quite so desperate, though precision and consistency of reasoning in such matters was admittedly not Arnold's forte. But it seems (as we shall see towards the end of this chapter) that Arnold had in mind a more general kind of heightened emotion, a rising above our ordinary selves, the kind of feeling that in his view poetry (we might feel inclined to say art more generally) has a particular capacity to arouse in us.

Such emotion inevitably brings with it a hovering awareness of something 'not ourselves'.

But this, of course, is already to begin to divest religion of any particular doctrinal content. There is a telling moment in *Literature and Dogma* when, in discussing what he sees as a false antithesis between natural and revealed religion, he says that 'religion springing out of an experience of the power, the grandeur, the necessity of righteousness is revealed religion, whether we find it in Sophocles or in Isaiah' (vi. 195). But this begs the whole question for the believer for whom the uniqueness of the Bible resides in the fact that it is the word of *God*, by comparison with which a work by some pagan dramatist has no standing, be it no matter how moving and effective in inciting us to righteousness (a highly contestable reading of the effect of a Sophoclean tragedy anyway).

Seen thus, Arnold's whole enterprise was anathema to the orthodox: it was bad enough to treat the Bible as a text like any other, worse still to treat it as a text by several authors. There was already, of course, a very considerable tradition of the so-called Higher Criticism of the Bible in the nineteenth century, though Arnold was irritated when people assimilated his work to that of the German scholars (for whom his esteem was limited), insisting that he was but developing the tendency of English Broad Church theology, with the aid of Spinoza (Arnold's protestations could not altogether hide the fact that his father, whose work he thus claimed to be continuing, had believed in a far more straightforward sense in the *truth* of Biblical revelation). Still, as the storm of controversy that greeted Jowett's contribution to *Essays and Reviews* in 1860 revealed, the application of ordinary standards of textual criticism to the Bible was far from being an accepted part of English intellectual life, and Arnold appeared to go much further than a liberal churchman like Jowett. Indeed, after the first two instalments had appeared as articles in the *Cornhill Magazine*, the editor decided against continuing the series, presumably for fear of too greatly offending the orthodox among his readers. As a consequence of this loss of his normal periodical outlet, *Literature and Dogma* is the only one of Arnold's major works that was actually written as a book.

But Arnold puzzled his readers, for he protested that he was trying to save 'the natural truth of Christianity', yet seemed to be setting aside all its distinctive doctrines. This, as well as Arnold's occasional preciosity, was wickedly caught in W. H. Mallock's satire, *The New Republic*, where he has the Arnold-figure, 'Mr Luke', say: 'It is true that culture sets aside the larger part of the New Testament as grotesque, barbarous and immoral; but what remains, purged of its apparent meaning, it discerns to be a treasure beyond all price.' There is shrewdness here, as there is in Lionel Trilling's later rhetorical question: 'Will men build Chartres to "a power not ourselves that makes for righteousness"?' Arnold wanted there to be religious emotion, but he wanted it to be stirred by things in which it is reasonable to believe; there may be loss as well as gain in this.

In *God and the Bible*, published two years later in 1875, Arnold responded to criticisms of *Literature and Dogma* and elaborated some of its themes further, but restatement only compounded his offence in the eyes of the orthodox. The book did reveal his surprising mastery of the technicalities of Biblical history and textual criticism, but it reiterated that this was all in the service of a practical goal, 'to restore the use of the Bible to those (and they are an increasing number) whom the popular theology with its proof from miracles, and the learned theology with its proof from metaphysics, so dissatisfy and repel that they are tempted to throw aside the Bible altogether' (vii. 143). Arnold took very seriously the task of making the Bible effective at the popular level. The establishment of compulsory elementary education by the Act of 1870 gave him a sense of urgency about the task: the Bible, he observed, is 'for the child in the elementary school almost his only contact with poetry and philosophy' (vii. 412). He therefore prepared a more accessible edition of the last 27 chapters of the Book of Isaiah in the Authorised Version as a Bible-reading for schools in 1872, and in 1883 he published his version of the first 66 chapters. That he should invest so much of the limited time available for his own writing in a project of this kind is itself an indication of the importance he attached to keeping alive some source of religious emotion for the unlearned masses, something that needs to be borne in mind in reading his writings on religion more generally.

A national institution

'A man who has published a good deal which is at variance with the body of theological doctrine commonly received in the Church of England and commonly preached by its ministers, cannot well, it may be thought, stand up before the clergy as a friend to their cause and to that of the Church' (viii. 65). But this is just what Arnold did, though evidently he could not altogether keep a smile out of his prose. In an address to Anglican clergymen, the author of *Literature and Dogma* explained why he valued the Established Church so highly. To be sure, his reasons were not their reasons: he called it 'a great national society for the promotion of goodness' (viii. 67), a playful use of the language of Victorian pressure-groups that no doubt grated on some of his clerical audience. But Arnold did genuinely value the Church of England, and it had a special place in his imaginative sympathies, both because it was a church and not a sect, and because it was the historic church of the English people. To some extent, his attachment was to an idealized Anglican Church rather than to the real thing, just as his reverence for Oxford was, in many ways, for an Oxford of the mind. He was well aware, and deplored, that, as he put it in 1871, Anglicanism's 'Tory, anti-democratic and even squirearchical character is very marked' (UL 57), and as he had drily observed some years earlier: 'It is not easy for a reflecting man, who has studied its origin, to feel any vehement enthusiasm for Anglicanism; Henry the Eighth and his parliaments have taken care of that' (ii, 320). None the less, he was true to his Broad Church, and hence ultimately Coleridgean, lineage in being convinced of the need for an established church as 'a beneficent social and civilising agent' (ii, 321).

Once again, Arnold's feeling for 'centrality' and 'comprehensiveness' manifested itself here. Those who are born within one of 'the great nationally established forms of religion' can 'get forward on their road, instead of always eyeing the ground on which they stand and disputing about it' (ii. 321); sharing its traditions and its discipline helps one 'to eschew self-assertion' (viii. 85). As the reference to 'forms' in the plural indicates, Arnold's argument was frankly cultural not theological: different churches were, for reasons of history and national character, suited to the

needs of different countries. The Anglican Church did not offer
the unique road to salvation; indeed, a too zealous insistence
on the exclusive doctrinal correctness of one's preferred religion
was the cloven hoof of sectarianism. But in England the Anglican
church had provided 'a shelter and basis for culture', and there
was still no agency that could rival its moral and aesthetic impact
upon the majority of the population.

The shape of Arnold's concern about this last aspect of the
Church's role is nicely illustrated in his discussion of an issue that
may now seem to be of barely antiquarian interest. Under legislation dating from the Restoration, Dissenters could only be buried
in English churchyards if the Anglican incumbent officiated, using
the service prescribed in the Book of Common Prayer. Dissenters
naturally pressed to be able to conduct their own services using
their own liturgy. Although Arnold was willing to make many
practical concessions to the Dissenters in an attempt to remove
their crippling sense of grievance and perhaps eventually in-
corporate them in the national church, he objected to Parliament
officially endorsing the use of the Dissenters' liturgy at public burial
services, because he placed great weight on the civilizing power of
the Church of England service on these public occasions. To make
his point, he compared the beauty of a passage from Milton with
that of a passage from Eliza Cook, a sentimental third-rate poet
popular with the Victorian middle-class. He conceded that there
was, of course, no sense in trying to compel people to read Milton
in private if they preferred Eliza Cook, 'yet Milton remains Milton,
and Eliza Cook remains Eliza Cook. And a public rite, with a
reading of Milton attached to it, is another thing from a public
rite with a reading from Eliza Cook' (viii. 345). Now, as Arnold
well knew, there was in fact no proposal by the Dissenters to use
Eliza Cook, nor, of course, did Milton figure in the Anglican
service, but what is so revealing about this example is that the
crucial division, in Arnold's mind, was *not* between the traditional
religious services of the two denominations on the one hand and
the poetry of the two poets on the other; for him, the important
distinction was between the beauties of the Anglican service and
Milton on the one hand, and the dreariness of the Dissenters'
service and Eliza Cook on the other.

For those disposed to be hostile to Arnold, his commitment to the Church of England seems particularly damning. Born of theological compromise and *raison d'état*, Anglicanism is derided as unspiritual, unsystematic, and irretrievably implicated in England's oligarchic social and political history. But Arnold did not require the condescension of later generations to make him aware that 'actual Anglicanism is certainly not Jerusalem' (ii. 321). However, for him as for the calmly unillusioned eighteenth-century divine, Bishop Butler, whom he so much admired, it was 'a *reasonable* Establishment', the existence of which encouraged that 'largeness of spirit' so lacking in all forms of sectarian self-importance. A 'vehement enthusiasm' was not what the Anglican Church excited in its more reflective members; indeed, 'vehement Anglicanism' may be an oxymoron. But then that, for Arnold, was not the least of its merits.

'*Joy whose grounds are true*'

In giving the title *Last Essays on Church and Religion* to the collection of pieces he published in 1877, Arnold signalled his intention of quitting the field of religious polemic. But in a sense, what really constituted his 'last essays' on religion, given the way he had re-defined religion, were his articles on literary subjects that he published in his final decade, above all his classic essays on 'Wordsworth', 'Byron', and 'The Study of Poetry'. In his late essays, Arnold comes very near to equating religion and poetry, partly because in both cases he views them pragmatically, in terms of the effect they have on us. Both do more than fortify and console, although, as we have already seen, this somewhat Stoic note tends to predominate in these essays; religion and poetry also animate and ennoble, and here the emphasis is on their effect on the will, on how they give us that energy and sense of purpose outside ourselves that enables us to meet the demands of morality. But even if the religious believer could accept this description of the psychological effect of his faith, still he would insist that it was consequential upon the *truth* of what he believed; for the believer, religion is not just an efficacious fiction. In what sense, it may be asked, can poetry lay claim to display any such truth? Some light is shed on this by, surprisingly, Arnold's essay on Byron (1881).

In the course of his usual attempt to fix a writer's position in the league tables of Poetic Greatness, Arnold's discussion of Byron requires a comparison between Leopardi and Wordsworth, and the conclusion to his argument for the ultimate superiority of the latter is particularly revealing.

It [his superiority] is in the power with which Wordsworth feels the resources of joy offered to us in nature, offered to us in the primary human affections and duties, and in the power with which, in his moments of inspiration, he renders this joy, and makes us, too, feel it; a force greater than himself seeming to lift him and to prompt his tongue, so that he speaks in a style far above any style of which he has the constant command, and with a truth far beyond any philosophic truth of which he has the conscious and assured possession. . . . As compared with Leopardi, Wordsworth, though at many points less lucid, though far less a master of style, far less of an artist, gains so much by his criticism of life being, in certain matters of profound importance, healthful and true, whereas Leopardi's pessimism is not, that the value of Wordsworth's poetry, on the whole, stands higher for us than that of Leopardi's. (ix. 230-1)

Here, Wordsworth's superiority initially seems to rest upon his capacity for positive feeling, his responsiveness to the sources of 'joy'. Whether this excludes any claims on behalf of his cognitive achievement, his clarity of perception about the human condition, depends upon whether we assume, as Arnold surely does, that Wordsworth's capacity to feel this joy is *itself* an index of the truth of his perception. Joy, rather than pain, is what a correctly-understood world has to offer. Something like this optimistic assumption seems to be present in the last sentence of the passage, where he asserts that Wordsworth's criticism of life is 'healthful and true, whereas Leopardi's pessimism is not'. The sense in which Leopardi's criticism of life is less 'true' than Wordsworth's doesn't seem to depend to any great extent upon an examination of what they actually say about the world, so much as upon a comparison of the effects they have upon the reader. The relation between the terms 'healthful' and 'true' in that passage is at least as much that it is true *because* healthful, as that it is healthful because true. To his pragmatic theory of poetry and religion, Arnold almost seems to be adding a pragmatic theory of truth here. As with his phrase 'joy whose grounds are true', it is not that he requires or proposes any very probing theory of the nature of reality to award the label 'true', but simply that what animates, what conduces to a state of mind in which there is a readiness for virtuous action, is what is true, and it is true because it in some way corresponds to our deepest feelings. And it is when these feelings are aroused, when our 'higher self' shakes itself free from the clutches of our appetite-satisfying 'lower self', that we rise to the level of moral conduct.

Despite his repeated assertions that 'conduct is three fourths of life' (conduct must have been index-linked to Arnold's growing earnestness, since it later became 'four fifths' of life), Arnold in the end had very little to say about morality, and he had very little to say about it because he essentially took it for granted. As he had put it, with bland confidence, in *Literature and Dogma*, 'conduct . . . is the simplest thing in the world as far as *understanding* is concerned; as regards *doing*, it is the hardest thing in the world' (vi. 172). For all his criticism of the 'prison of Puritanism' from which English life had yet to escape, his work does not really contain much critical engagement with the actual moral code of his day, as opposed to the spirit in which that morality was intruded into all discussion. What he is preoccupied with, instead, is getting people to live up to the moral code, finding a source of emotion, a prompt for strong *feeling*. Ultimately, he, like so many of his contemporaries, appears to be secure in the confidence that those feelings will be harmonious, both with each other and with the feelings and needs of other people.

The note of melancholy characteristic of Arnold's best poetry, the voice of a self observing its need for a faith it cannot believe, and expressing the sadness that this awareness of perpetual frustration must induce, is largely absent from his later writings on literature and religion. He now seems more confident that the Bible *does* meet our needs, that poetry *is* our 'stay'. This is largely because he is here addressing the needs (the rather limited needs, as he conceives of them) of the mass of the population for emotional sustenance and moral guidance, rather than singing of the plight of the over-reflective individual. But perhaps it is also true that, as in some of his other writing of this period, there is detectable a slight hardening or coarsening of Arnold's thought in the last decade of his life, or at least more of a tendency to paint in the great primary colours and to insist on the preaching of certain large and simple truths. It is noticeable, too, that his religious writings are far less ironical and facetious in tone, and, with the exception of his notorious trope of 'the three Lord Shaftesburys' to illustrate the popular idea of the Trinity (which he later removed), these writings have little of that high-spirited banter that some readers of his earlier works found offensive.

Although a string of Modernist theologians and, more recently, several literary critics of the Bible have paid tribute to Arnold's religious writings, most modern readers have found them the least satisfying part of his work. In his effort to salvage Christianity from the popular theology and Biblical literalism of his day, he now looks like a man who has retreated to a higher sand-castle to escape a wave without realizing that the tide will soon engulf sand-castle and beach as well. And yet, as a suggestion of where future generations might look to find what their less troubled predecessors had found in traditional Christianity, his work may not have fared so badly after all. Arguably, many people, without ever putting it in Arnold's terms, do find a source of moral guidance and sense of 'something not ourselves' in art if they find it anywhere; more, perhaps, in genres like novels and films than in poetry and tragedy in their traditional forms. A passage from the eighteenth-century German writer Herder, which Arnold copied into his notebooks, may stand for much informal twentieth-century belief: 'It is culture [*Bildung*] alone which binds together the generations which live one after another as men who see but one day, and it is in culture that the solidarity of mankind is to be sought, since in it the strivings of all men coincide.'

In his desire to preserve the greatest possible cultural continuity and his looking to literature for moral authority, as, more obviously, in his responsiveness to the beauties of the King James Bible and his affection for the curious growth that is Anglicanism, Arnold seems a very distinctively English writer. (Certainly, European critics, normally so appreciative of his cosmopolitan range, greeted his religious writings with a kind of baffled respect.) This thought may have been in the mind of his friend, Grant Duff, when in 1889 he recorded in his diary having attended a meeting about a memorial fund for Arnold that had taken place in the Jerusalem Chamber of Westminster Abbey:

How strange amidst all its revolutions is the continuousness of England! Here were we assembled in a room which was historical long before Shakespeare, and made world-famous by him,—to do what? In the very place in which the Westminster divines had set forth in elaborate propositions the curious form of nonsense which was Christianity to them, to do honour to a man who, standing quite outside their dogmas, had seen more deeply into the heart of the matter than all of them put together.

7 The Arnoldian legacy

It is a remarkable fact that Matthew Arnold is more central to the cultural debates of the late twentieth century than he has been at any time in the hundred years since his death. It would seem eccentric, or at least obsessively academic, to attempt to register one's present intellectual or political allegiances by hoisting a flag marked, say, 'Carlyle' or 'Ruskin', for all that one might feel admiration for their achievements or sympathy with their ideas; those names simply do not denominate a readily recognizable identity for current controversial purposes. But 'Arnold', and still more the conveniently unspecific 'Arnoldian', is widely taken to signal a claim to descent and an affirmation of loyalty from which one's response to a variety of still-contested issues could be fairly accurately inferred. This may seem simply to provide further testimony to his continued vitality and readability: for all their constant allusion to the now-forgotten polemics of Victorian England, the best of his writings could be said to have dated less than those of any of his peers, with the possible exception of John Stuart Mill. But for a less naïvely individualistic explanation of his talismanic role, we need to consider the vagaries of his reputation in the past century, and, even more, to recognize how a pattern of cultural change has thrust a certain representative status upon him.

At the time of his death in 1888, Arnold already stood in a slightly uneasy relation to the first members of that diverse and fractious brood who claimed to be his rightful literary descendants. Most notably, there was the doubtful and ambiguous case of the various strands that made up the late nineteenth-century movement commonly called 'aestheticism'; figures as diverse as Walter Pater, Oscar Wilde, and Max Beerbohm could all be seen as having absconded with part of his legacy, and imitation of one aspect of Arnold's style (much diluted and mixed with two parts mannerism to one part talent) coloured the somewhat precious and whimsical literary 'portraits' and 'appreciations' produced by the next generation of velveteen-jacketed Edwardian bookmen. Of course, in the complex manner of intellectual history, this development can be seen both as a continuation of, but also as the beginning of a reaction against, some of those features least inaccurately described as 'Victorian' (and the complexity is multiplied because Arnold himself was in some ways a Victorian critic of aspects of what came to be known as 'Victorianism').

The generation or two after a writer's death usually sees the trough of his reputation, and in Arnold's case this was intensified by the voguish rejection of all things 'Victorian' in the first three or four decades of the twentieth century. Lytton Strachey, for example, contributed a routinely abusive essay on Arnold just before the First World War, refusing to see anything but the heavy moralism and enlarged social conscience of the later Arnold which Strachey's polemical parody of 'Victorianism' required, wilfully ignoring the urbanity, wit, and taste for French literature which, in altered forms, were so essential to Strachey's sense of his own identity. (The cardinal document of the 'reaction against Victorianism', Strachey's *Eminent Victorians*, with its sinuously insinuating portrait of Arnold's father, followed four years later in 1918.) Only in the 1940s did this kind of cultural Oedipal antagonism cease to dominate responses to the great public figures of the late nineteenth century.

On another plane, the prejudices of literary 'Modernism' were hostile to the spoilt Romanticism of the mainstream of Victorian verse. At the beginning of the century, Arnold had been held in special affection and respect by what one might call 'the Golden Treasury view' of English verse; a selection of his poetry *had* been edited by Sir Arthur Quiller-Couch, after all. When the tide of literary fashion turned against this, the audience for Arnold's poetry, which was anyway never wide, contracted still further. Described as 'after Milton, the most learned of English poets', Arnold has naturally attracted extensive academic annotation and commentary in recent years, and it is this which has largely restored his standing as a poet.

Although the reputation of Arnold's prose was at its nadir in the first few decades of this century, he remained an inescapable presence in both Britain and the United States. But to understand the nature of the peculiar significance that he has since acquired, it is crucial to recognize that his authority was most loudly invoked in the 1920s and 1930s by those who emphasized the social role of literature as an agent of cultural regeneration in the face of what was stigmatized as 'mass civilization'. In Britain, the very influential 'Newbolt Report' on 'The Teaching of English', which appeared in 1921, was an explicitly Arnoldian document, injecting an upbeat version of his 'message' into the curriculum of the next generation. But far more important for his long-term standing was the fact that the three writers who did most to install literary criticism in its central position in modern British culture all explicitly associated Arnold with the larger moral and political purposes of their enterprise. For all the self-justifyingly distancing tone of some of their remarks about Arnold, and for all the very great differences between each of them as well as between any one of them and Arnold, it remains true that through the writings in the 1920s and 1930s of T. S. Eliot, I. A. Richards, and F. R. Leavis, his name was thenceforth associated with their distinctively twentieth-century programme of cultural renewal.

Although this development was particularly intimately intertwined with the intricacies of English social and intellectual life, the appropriation of Arnold by later social critics who found something superficially congenial in his style and concerns was to some extent a significant episode in American cultural history also. For example, the 'Humanism' of Irving Babbitt and his followers in the first few decades of the twentieth century explicitly traced its descent back to Arnold, thus encouraging an identification of his work with an anxiously reactionary response to the democratization of modern societies. More influential in the long run, however, was the publication in 1939 of Lionel Trilling's *Matthew Arnold*, which not only introduced a more serious and sympathetic appraisal of Arnold's ideas, but also, by the affinity it suggested between its subject and its author—who was to become the outstanding American critic in the three decades after the Second World War, a critic of comparably wide intellectual interests and not dissimilar cultural convictions—helped bring Arnold into prominence in post-war literary-political debates in the United States also.

But from this point, Arnold's increasing significance has to be seen in relation to the wider developments I alluded to earlier. The most important of these have been, first, the enormous growth of higher education since the end of the nineteenth century, which has in turn led to the cultural concerns of modern societies being far more intimately tied to academic fashions and controversies than ever before, and, secondly, a remarkable expansion of the teaching of English literature in universities during the last fifty years. When Arnold died, 'Eng. Lit.' was practically unknown as an academic subject (as, of course, were several others that have since attained that dubious respectability); now, it is often the largest single humanities department in British and American universities. But more important than sheer expansion of numbers has been the fact that literary studies have borne the double burden of aspiring to some recognized disciplinary status, possessing its own techniques and vocabulary, while at the same time providing a forum and an idiom in which larger moral and existential questions can be broached. This has nourished, and has in turn fed on, the large cultural hopes invested in 'English' as the successor-subject to Classics, and even as the successor-religion to Christianity. As one observer has put it: 'True to Arnold's prophecy, literature has become the religion of the twentieth century, with criticism its theology.'

Like so many others, Arnold has thus had academic greatness thrust upon him. Despite his sentimental fondness for an idealized Oxford, he was not in the least an academic critic. Moreover, he was sceptical about some of the proposals for the introduction of literature into the university syllabus that were advanced towards the end of his life, urging, for example, that English literature should certainly not be taught in isolation from its Classical and European sources. But, despite the fact that he never confined his notion of 'criticism' exclusively to *literary* criticism, just as the literature he recommended was not primarily *English* literature, Arnold was the chief of those recruited to preside over and give legitimacy to a new professional specialism. Furthermore, the fact that, for various reasons, literary criticism in Britain continued to use, as to some extent it still does, that informal, conversational register which Arnold recommended and exemplified, has in effect disguised the extent to which modern literary scholarship has moved away from the assumptions that sustained the judgements of a cultivated and discriminating man of letters in the mid-nineteenth century.

None the less, until about 1960 it continued to be possible to believe that the dominant forms of 'criticism' carried on within university departments of English (whose influence on the wider culture was by this date attracting much comment) still belonged within a tradition that could, without too much violence to the facts, be traced back to Arnold more than to any other single figure. Since then, of course, there has been a quick succession of critical 'new waves' which have promised both to provide a properly scientific methodology for a discipline still troubled by its doubtful standing, and at the same time to entail a set of more unambiguously radical political conclusions. The oddity of the yoking together of these two not obviously compatible aspirations is a reminder of how even the most iconoclastic critical theories have continued to assume the dual burden that the needs of twentieth-century culture have imposed on the study and teaching of literature. Partly for this reason, and partly because of the traditionally close links between literature and 'the higher journalism' in Britain and to a lesser extent the United States, these disputes have attracted a degree of public attention not lavished on the internal squabbles of any other academic discipline.

It is not difficult to see how Arnold has constituted a convenient target for those who pride themselves on being both methodological and political radicals, and in recent decades he has come in for some pretty rough handling. Of course, all earlier critics can, if treated with the right mixture of animosity and high-handedness, be made to look intellectually naïve by their more self-consciously sophisticated successors. Though there might seem to be some intellectual, and certainly some professional, advantage to be gained from exposing the questionable assumptions underlying the work of, say, Dryden or Johnson, there would seem to be little cultural payoff to 'unmasking' the way these assumptions were rooted in political or moral beliefs that are no longer considered acceptable (this does not, however, mean that no one ever does it). But the sense of greater direct continuity with

Arnold's concerns, and a suspicion that current critical practices still draw authority from, and are to some extent based on, his canonical pronouncements, means that 'unmasking' *his* assumptions in this way can seem a worthwhile victory, the slaying of a father who would otherwise exercise a tyrannical authority.

Arnold has not been without his champions, of course: the founding in the 1950s of a journal with the deliberately Arnoldian title of *Essays in Criticism*, for example, made the assumed line of descent explicit, and as this line has come under increasingly severe attack in recent decades, some of those who have styled themselves its defenders have invoked Arnold as a talisman against the evil demons suspected of lurking down the departmental corridor. All this has not necessarily resulted in any greater or more sympathetic understanding of his work, but it has undeniably kept his name, though sometimes little else, at the centre of those debates in which some of the sharpest divisions in modern intellectual life have been expressed.

But Arnold resonates within a wider field of conflict still, particularly in Britain, and this involves a further aspect of the broader historical developments I mentioned above. The dispute here is ultimately political: the social changes of the mid-twentieth century, the wider recruitment to higher education not least among them, have issued in an assault on the assumptions behind the traditional position of what has come to be called, usually pejoratively, 'high culture'. The gist of the many charges that cluster around this topic is that the prescriptive ideal of 'culture', and especially the limited specification of its content, derives from and reinforces a pattern of relations between classes, sexes, and races that is fundamentally unjust. This charge has appeared in its most uncompromising form as part of the class antagonisms that have set the agenda for much modern British political and, to a lesser extent, intellectual history (and which have therefore given that history some of the intensity, but also opacity to outsiders, that characterizes the family quarrel). Along with this rejection of the value and standing of the traditional conception of culture has gone a dismissal of any notion of 'cultural centrality', which is scorned as the imposition of the limited preoccupations of a privileged élite upon the rival and no less legitimate concerns of other social groups. An equally hostile treatment, on similar grounds, has been given to the very idea of a 'canon' of particularly valuable or inescapably major works of art and literature, a hostility which in turn has sometimes led to a revision, or more usually an expansion, of the categories of 'art' and 'literature' themselves.

Naturally, Arnold presents himself as a particularly inviting target here, too. Not only did he decisively shape the modern prescriptive notion of 'culture', but he also explicitly promoted its capacity to heal ('suppress', according to the more intransigent) social conflicts, an ideal discernible only just below the surface of much educational thinking and activity in twentieth-century Britain. Moreover, as we saw in Chapter 5, he exhibited a strong attachment to 'order', and urged a more elevated conception of the state; he spoke favourably of the role in diffusing culture to be played by those 'aliens' outside the three classes; and, in more historical detail, he was less than implacably hostile to the established order—he was indulgent to the Anglican Church, for instance, and was known to have hob-nobbed with the titled and landed, all of which has been cited as casting doubt on the value of his ideas. Even so distinguished a critic as Raymond Williams, to take an influential example, felt it important to try to discredit Arnold by showing that his response to the Hyde Park riots of 1866 was not the 'correct' one. As I implied a moment ago, there would surely be something laughable about taking great pains to reveal that Dryden's assumptions were insufficiently 'democratic' or that Johnson's were reprehensibly 'ethnocentric', yet Arnold has had to face several such firing-squads at successive new political dawns.

It is noticeable, too, that Arnold attracts a particular rage of resentment not just because of what he can be accused of 'standing for', but also because of the very poise and grace with which he conducted himself. This, in turn, is partly because these qualities themselves are now frequently subject to the suspicion of being obstructive affectations, but also perhaps because unless guarded against, their seductive appeal may still do some of its work of sapping dogmatism and reducing exaggeration. The rage may be involuntary tribute to his power: the resentment is redoubled by an irritation that the despised qualities should still be able to exert any pull over us. In any event, for many cultural commentators today he has become, in a telling appropriation of his own term, 'a negative touchstone'.

By this point it will have become obvious that some of the reasons for Arnold's current importance bear only a tenuous relation to any considered understanding of the complexities of his tone and temper. Yet it is by those qualities of balance, perceptiveness, and wit, which he sometimes embodied as well as recommended, that he provides a still-effective antidote to just that cast of mind that insists on denigrating him for its own partisan purposes. One unfortunate outcome of the linked historical developments discussed above is that any attempt at a reasonably dispassionate assessment of his achievement, something which presupposes a measure of imaginative sympathy and sensitivity to the historical constraints of his situation, runs a high risk of having covertly sectarian motives ascribed to it.

Needless to say, not even Arnold's most devoted champions (of whom I am not one) could acquit him of *all* the charges that have been laid against him over the years, and I hope the previous chapters of this book have sufficiently indicated where I think he is most liable to criticism. In general, it would have to be allowed that he did not altogether practise what he preached: disinterestedness too often gave way to self-indulgence or unfairness, for example. Moreover, we need be under no illusion that what he preached, even taken at its best, adds up to an adequate diet. His work, the poetry included, does not really touch the extremes of human life: he can be pessimistic but he does not rise to the tragic; he can be joyful without ever reaching the sublime. It is not that he did not know almost unbearably painful suffering, nor that he underestimated its place in human life; but such matters did not find unforgettable expression in his writing. Viewed from another perspective, of course, one can be grateful that these matters did not monopolize his attention, and that he does not try to force them to monopolize ours; it is hardly a complaint to observe that the characteristic tone of his best prose can have an almost Mozartian gaiety about it.

Some, both among his contemporaries and ours, have been suspicious of the habitual balance of his tone, and have seen something a little too willed in what Hutton called his 'imperious serenity'.

But if a form of composure or equanimity is achieved without undue suppression, it is not obvious that we should value it the less for the fact that it is *achieved* rather than natural. A misplaced cult of authenticity may encourage particular intolerance of a self-conscious stylist like Arnold, in whom we have to recognize a continuity between the stylishness of his writing and the accomplished (in both senses of the word) balance of his character.

This balance may have limited both the range and register of Arnold's writing. To adopt his own favoured comparative way of speaking, we may say that he does not give us the huge canvas and black passions of, say, a Dostoevsky, or the unnerving brilliance and spiky originality of a Nietzsche, or the moral passion and architectonic power of a Marx. In citing such names we are only following his own practice of always placing the writer he is assessing in the company of the indisputably outstanding, to keep our assessments in perspective. There was in Arnold, to repeat that perceptive phrase of Charlotte Brontë's, 'a real modesty beneath the assumed conceit', and he would not have wanted his own standing to be allowed to get out of proportion.

'Perspective' and 'proportion' call to mind the cooler virtues, and that is right. If in the end we are persuaded and buoyed up by reading Arnold's best prose, it is surely because we know that the lightness of touch and the feel for style, no less than his actual convictions on culture and conduct, do embody a deeply pondered response to the place of these things in the larger scheme of life. It is not, of course, a complete response, and not always the response we most want or even need, but it is surely an indispensable element in any adequately receptive view of what the variousness of our literary heritage can offer us. The Mozartian parallel should not be overworked (proportion might even compel us to substitute, let us say, Rossini), but even the mere mention of it can remind us that there has to be cheerfulness and amenity as well as drama and justice if life is to be managed at all.

However, despite Arnold's early commendation of 'the grand style', to end on a note of anything like portentousness would be the least appropriate way to do justice to his continuing appeal. With a writer who 'perceived so many shy truths . . .', the tone of our leave-taking should have some of the intimacy and informality he so winningly cultivated in the two genres in which he excelled, the meditative lyric and the conversational essay. An occasional piece, composed in a minor key, may suggest a more suitable register. The poet who felt so deeply that 'we mortal millions live *alone*' was also exceptionally responsive to the consolations offered by that sense of kinship, transcending our own isolation and transience, which we can sometimes experience when a writer speaks to us across the chasm of centuries in a voice that we recognize as both like and unlike our own. In 1877 Arnold published his affectionate appreciation of Falkland, the seventeenth-century statesman and man of letters who found himself caught between the insistent simplicities of the two sides in the English Civil War. Arnold, himself more ambivalent Cavalier than ardent Roundhead, obviously felt some sympathy with this sensitive man trapped by the movement of history, with 'the lucidity of mind and largeness of temper' to see that he would be forced to give himself to 'the least bad of two unsound causes' (viii. 204). Occurring as it does in the middle of a fairly slight periodical essay on by no means the most important figure in English seventeenth-century history, his reflection on this fate provides a suitable note on which to take leave of Arnold himself.

Shall we blame him for his lucidity of mind and largeness of temper? Shall we even pity him? By no means. They are his great title to our veneration. They are what make him ours; what link him with the nineteenth century. He . . . by [his] heroic and hopeless stand against the inadequate ideals dominant in [his] time, kept open [his] communications with the future, lived with the future. [His] battle is ours too.

Further reading

The editions of Arnold's prose and poetry by R. H. Super and
Kenneth Allott respectively (details of which are given in the note
at the beginning of this book) not only establish the authoritative
texts of his works and record textual variants, but also provide a
great deal of useful historical, critical, and bibliographical information. They are now the indispensable starting-points for the
serious study of Arnold, and I have relied upon them heavily.
Selections from Arnold's writings are available in various modern
editions: three of the most accessible are *Matthew Arnold: Selected
Prose*, edited by P. J. Keating in the Penguin English Library
(Harmondsworth, 1970; repr. 1982); *Arnold: Poems*, selected by
Kenneth Allott in the Penguin Poetry Library (Harmondsworth,
1954; repr. with new Introduction by Jenni Calder, 1971; repr.
1985); and *Matthew Arnold: Selected Works*, edited by Miriam Allott
and R. H. Super in the Oxford Authors series (Oxford, 1986). The
various editions of his letters and notebooks are also cited at the
beginning of this book; the two-volume collection of letters edited in
1895 by G. W. E. Russell remains the most important biographical
source, though it is seriously inadequate in several ways, not least
in its unacknowledged excisions from some letters. A considerable
number of Arnold's letters have come to light in the past century:
copies of nearly all of them are now held at the University of
Virginia at Charlottesville, where a complete edition is being prepared under the direction of Cecil Lang. Much the fullest biography, which draws extensively on these sources, is now Park
Honan, *Matthew Arnold: a Life* (London, 1981).

There is a vast secondary literature on Arnold, and what follows
is a very brief selection, containing those works that I have
found particularly useful or stimulating. For fuller and more
authoritative guides, one should consult David J. DeLaura (ed.),
Victorian Prose: A Guide to Research (New York, 1973); Frederic E.
Faverty (ed.), *The Victorian Poets: A Guide to Research* (Cambridge,

Mass., 1956; 2nd edn. 1968); and the annual bibliographies provided in three periodicals: *Victorian Studies*, *Victorian Poetry*, and *The Arnoldian*. Some indication of the range of contemporary response to Arnold may be gathered from the relevant volumes in the 'Critical Heritage' series: *Matthew Arnold: the Poetry*, edited by Carl Dawson (London, 1973), and *Matthew Arnold: Prose Writings*, edited by Carl Dawson and John Pfordresher (London, 1979).

The most interesting book-length study of Arnold remains, in my view, Lionel Trilling's *Matthew Arnold* (New York, 1939; repr. Oxford, 1982); the sections on the historical context now seem a little superficial, and the treatment of both the poetry and the religious writings is perhaps rather thin in places, but the book is the expression of a genuine and impressive meeting of minds. Two particularly good collections of essays on Arnold, which deal with both the poetry and the prose, are David J. DeLaura (ed.), *Matthew Arnold: a Collection of Critical Essays* (Englewood Cliffs, N. J., 1973) and Kenneth Allott (ed.), *Matthew Arnold*, 'Writers and their Background', (London, 1975).

On the poetry, the most comprehensive discussion is A. Dwight Culler, *Imaginative Reason: The Poetry of Matthew Arnold* (New Haven, 1966). Also of interest in different ways are Louis Bonnerot, *Matthew Arnold, poète* (Paris, 1947); G. Robert Stange, *Matthew Arnold: The Poet as Humanist* (Princeton, 1967); and the chapter on Arnold in J. Hillis Miller, *The Disappearance of God: Five Nineteenth-Century Writers* (Cambridge Mass., 1963; 2nd edn. 1975). C. B. Tinker and H. F. Lowry, *The Poetry of Matthew Arnold: a Commentary* (London, 1940) is still useful.

Certain aspects of Arnold's thought and prose have been the subject of some outstandingly good scholarship, others rather less so. Sidney Coulling, *Matthew Arnold and his Critics: A Study of Arnold's Controversies* (Athens, Ohio, 1974) is excellent and immensely useful; David J. DeLaura, *Hebrew and Hellene in Victorian England: Newman, Arnold, Pater* (Austin, Texas, 1969) is a distinguished study; the chapter on Arnold in John Holloway, *The Victorian Sage: Studies in Argument* (London, 1953) is extremely perceptive. Arnold's literary and cultural criticism has been the subject of several classic essays (reprinted in the collections of essays cited above); two books which are interesting and very learned, but which perhaps ride their particular interpretations a little hard, are William A. Madden, *Matthew Arnold: A Study of the Aesthetic Temperament in Victorian England* (Bloomington, 1967) and Joseph Carroll, *The Cultural Theory of Matthew Arnold* (Berkeley, 1982). His social and political writings have been rather poorly served: F. G. Walcott, *The Origins of 'Culture and Anarchy'* (London, 1970) is useful on Arnold's educational writings in the 1860s, but Patrick J. McCarthy, *Matthew Arnold and the Three Classes* (New York, 1964) is disappointing. Arnold's religious and moral thought has been discussed very thoroughly in William Robbins, *The Ethical Idealism of Matthew Arnold: A Study of the Nature and Sources of his Moral Ideas* (Toronto, 1959), in the chapters on Arnold in Vincent Buckley, *Poetry and Morality* (London, 1959), and in Ruth apRoberts, *Arnold and God* (Berkeley, 1983).

Notes on sources

My chief scholarly debts are acknowledged in the note on Further Reading. The sources of actual quotations given in the text, other than from Arnold's works, are as follows.

7. 'imperious serenity'. R. H. Hutton, *Literary Essays* (London, 1888), p. 317.

10. '. . . of my enemies'. Leslie Stephen, quoted in David J. DeLaura, *Victorian Prose: A Guide to Research* (New York, 1973), p. 290.

10. '. . . enormously insulting'. G. K. Chesterton, quoted in DeLaura, *Victorian Prose*, p. 290.

10. '. . . lizard slickness'. Geoffrey Tillotson, *Criticism and the Nineteenth Century* (London, 1951), p. 56.

16. 'high-hat persiflage'. Tillotson, *Criticism and the Nineteenth Century*, p. 49.

17. '. . . of insensibility'. Henry James, 'Matthew Arnold' (1884), repr. in Henry James, *Literary Criticism*, Vol. 1 (New York, 1984), pp. 728, 731.

23. '. . . ourselves, poetry'. W. B. Yeats, quoted in Edward Alexander, 'Roles of the Victorian Critic', in P. Damon (ed.), *Literary Criticism and Historical Understanding* (New York, 1967), p. 53.

23. '. . . assumed conceit'. Charlotte Brontë, quoted in Park Honan, *Matthew Arnold, A Life* (London, 1981), p. 220.

24. '. . . ever known'. E. Abbott and L. Campbell, *The Life and Letters of Benjamin Jowett*, Vol. 1 (London 1897), p. 223.

27. '. . . in the world'. A. Dwight Culler, *Imaginative Reason: The Poetry of Matthew Arnold* (New Haven, 1966), p. 4.

29. 'time-ridden consciousness'. William A. Madden, *Matthew Arnold: A Study of the Aesthetic Temperament in Victorian England* (Bloomington, 1967), p. 83.

39. '. . . the body gone?'. A. C. Swinburne, quoted in Frederic E. Faverty (ed.), *The Victorian Poets: A Guide to Research* (Cambridge, Mass., 1956; 2nd edn. 1968), p. 200.

41-2. '. . . Virgilian regret', and '. . . does not know', both Hutton, *Literary Essays*, pp. 352, 350.

43. '. . . heroic egotism'. Hutton, *Literary Essays*, p. 313.

46. '. . . than a critic'. T. S. Eliot, *The Sacred Wood* (London, 1920), p. 1.

46. '. . . literary criticism'. F. R. Leavis, 'Arnold as Critic' (1938), repr. in F. R. Leavis, *The Critic as Anti-Philosopher*, ed. G. Singh (London, 1982), p. 57.

47. '. . . resign himself to . . .'. J. A. Froude, quoted in Howard Foster Lowry (ed.), *The Letters of Matthew Arnold to Arthur Hugh Clough* (London, 1932), p. 127.

66. 'doomsday standards'. Tillotson, *Criticism and the Nineteenth Century*, p. 80.

67. '. . . felt his impact'. Honan, *Matthew Arnold*, p. viii.

84. 'Greeker than thou'. Richard Jenkyns, *The Victorians and Ancient Greece* (Oxford, 1980), p. 265.

94. '. . . Christian at bottom'. Quoted in Basil Willey, 'Arnold and Religion', in Kenneth Allott (ed.), *Matthew Arnold* (London, 1975), p. 236.

102. '. . . beyond all price'. W. H. Mallock, *The New Republic: Culture, Faith and Philosophy in an English Country-House* (London, 1877; repr. Leicester, 1975), p. 31.

102. '". . . makes for righteousness"?'. Lionel Trilling, *Matthew Arnold* (New York, 1939; repr. Oxford, 1982), p. 321.

108. '. . . all men coincide'. Quoted (and identified) in Ruth apRoberts, *Arnold and God* (Berkeley, 1983), p. 45.

109. '. . . them put together'. Quoted in Sidney M. B. Coulling, *Matthew Arnold and his Critics: A Study of Arnold's Controversies* (Athens, Ohio, 1974), p. 268.

113. '. . . criticism its theology'. David Lodge, 'Literary Criticism in England in the Twentieth Century', in Bernard Bergonzi (ed.), *The Twentieth Century* (The Pelican Guide to English Literature) (Harmondsworth, 1970), p. 372.

116. 'correct'. Raymond Williams, *Politics and Letters* (London, 1979), p. 124.

Afterword to the Clarendon Paperback Edition

The first edition of this book was published in the Oxford University Press 'Past Masters' series. In that form, flanked by similar volumes on comparable figures, its nature was clear and required neither explanation nor justification. Of course, any such introductory book involves an element of artifice on the part of the writer, who must affect a kind of innocence: information and interpretation must be offered in confident and accessible terms while silently suppressing the clamour of qualification and contention with which scholars in the field might greet almost every statement. It is also true that with a short book, written to a prescribed length, the most significant decisions are those of proportion and omission, decisions that are virtually invisible to the uninstructed eye. But even when critics take issue with the specific emphases and lacunae of such a portrait, they thereby signal their acceptance of the aspiration to produce a likeness, and in general the constraints of the genre are acknowledged and accepted.

It would seem, however, that there are at present special hazards involved in attempting such an estimate of Arnold, special charges of tendentiousness or partisanship that one is likely to incur, and it may be worth reflecting on these as a way of considering his continuing significance. As I suggest in Chapter 7, comparable studies of figures such as, say, Dryden or Johnson (to mention simply a couple of Arnold's great predecessors as critics) might attract scholarly grumbles over this or that disputed interpretation, but the mere fact of attending to that particular writer would not be taken as a wide-ranging declaration of cultural and political allegiances. To venture an assessment of Arnold, however, is to encounter a different level of response: one is assumed to be taking up a stance on a cultural battleground. It is a nice question which of the two main responses one is there liable to meet is the more distasteful—being vilified for failing to endorse truths one does not wish to deny, or being enfolded in the warm embrace of those whose attitudes one does not share.

Arnold, it is clear, retains his vitality as a vehicle, or at times only an occasion, for controversy. In my concluding chapter I remark that Arnold is now more 'central' than at any time since his death. This has been disputed on the grounds that Arnold had more disciples in the 1930s and 1940s when his reputation was revived by leading critics like F. R. Leavis and Lionel Trilling, and that 'Arnoldians' are now a straggling 'remnant'.[1] But while this may accurately describe part of the curve of Arnold's popularity, we must be careful to distinguish centrality from endorsement. Arnold is central now in the sense that I mentioned in the previous paragraph: he stands at the centre of a series of debates. Many who contribute to those debates, as I have suggested, are severely critical of Arnold, but that is a different matter: they still attend to him, or at least to a straw-man of that name. This has something to do with features of his tone and manner of writing that have always provoked and either charmed or irritated his readers (these are the features I try particularly to address in Chapter 1). But beyond this, as I argue in the final chapter, there are circumstances specific to the late-twentieth century which conspire to thrust attention on his name, attention which is different in kind from that directed at his writings in the first two or three generations after his death. Chief among these circumstances are, first, the attack, from various quarters, on any unitary or exclusive conception of culture; second, the burden of moral sustenance placed upon the study and teaching of literature; and third, the spread of a theoretically grounded scepticism about the very possibility of 'disinterestedness'. The contexts in which Arnold's name has been invoked, revered, and denigrated in the past six years suggest that these themes continue to be the main determinants of the function of Arnold at the present time.

Indeed, in recent years there has been an intensification of some of these polemics in ways that have directly affected Arnold's general standing and relevance. Two developments have been particularly significant here. The first is that both Britain and America have been swept by a strong current of cultural conservatism in the 1980s, often drawing upon powerful governmental support, which has attempted to reassert the value and centrality of what it regards as the canonical cultural monuments in the face of the more 'progressive' or relativist

---

[1] Chris Baldick, 'A Question of Centrality', *TLS* (13 Jan. 1989), 43.

ideas that flourished in the 1960s and 1970s. And the second is that the source of the most fashionable challenges to the traditional notion of the study of English literature is now less likely to be characterized as coming from 'literary theory' than from 'cultural studies'. It will immediately be obvious that these developments have not diminished Arnold's centrality.

Perhaps no single event better illustrated how Arnold's name had acquired totemic significance in disputes about 'culture' than the publication in 1984 of a report entitled *To Reclaim a Legacy*, written by William J. Bennett, at the time the Director of the major federal agency for funding research in the humanities in the United States, the National Endowment for the Humanities (Bennett was later promoted by President Reagan to be the Secretary for Education). In the spirit of its title, the report was an aggressively conservative reassertion of the values of what it took to be the traditional landmarks of Western culture, a heritage it attempted to characterize in terms borrowed from Arnold: 'Expanding a phrase from Matthew Arnold, I would describe the humanities as the best that has been said, thought, written, and otherwise expressed about the human experience' (the doubling of Arnold's already past-tense verbs only underlined the report's conservatism). The powerful strategic position of the report's author was one reason why these sentiments received such close, and from academics usually hostile, scrutiny: the expression of such convictions in funding policies threatened to be highly consequential. But these ideas continued to receive attention also because they came to be associated with the furore surrounding two unlikely best-sellers later in the decade, Allan Bloom's *The Closing of the American Mind: How Higher Education Has Failed Democracy and Impoverished the Souls of Today's Students* (1988), and E. D. Hirsch Jr.'s *Cultural Literacy: What Every American Needs to Know* (1987). These books were widely perceived as representing a conservative cultural backlash—one observer described Bloom and Hirsch as 'in some aspects of their work, blustering reactionaries'.[2] One of the unfortunate effects of their attempted appropriation of one version of the Arnoldian legacy has been to make it too easy to dismiss anybody who has a sympathetic word to say about Arnold as helping

---

[2] John P. Farrell, 'Matthew Arnold: The Writer as Touchstone', *Victorian Poetry*, 26 (1989), 8.

to nourish this kind of combative conservatism. Roughly speaking, this all made it easier to believe that condemning the author of *Culture and Anarchy* was a vital pre-condition for being able to continue to teach feminist theory or black studies from a base in an English department.

This, in turn, relates to the second development mentioned above, namely the sudden popularity of that congeries of approaches, themselves far from wholly novel, termed 'cultural studies'. Although the nature and justification of the teaching of literature has certainly continued to be the subject of heated debate, the high-point of the 'theory-wars' of the 1970s and early 1980s seems to have passed. None the less, the more radically inclined contributors to these discussions, those who wish to displace both terms in the traditional category of 'English Literature', have continued to identify Arnold as the 'founding father for conventional English studies',[3] seeing him as 'largely responsible for the establishing of that discipline of "English", the transformation of which is contemporary literary theory's acknowledged mission', and hence as 'a master-strategist in the formation of a hegemonic cultural discourse'.[4] Indeed, whereas in the wider society it tends to be those who want to endorse what they think Arnold represents who are keenest to mention him, in the academic world it is those who wish to disparage what they believe to have been Arnold's role who have done most to keep his name in the professional headlines. (In Britain these debates have in recent years been given an added realism and concreteness by being linked to the question of the teaching of literature in schools and its place in the new National Curriculum). This hostile stereotyping is one of the pressures that has made it difficult for assessments of Arnold's strengths and weaknesses to escape partisan labelling, but there are welcome signs that he may be being emancipated from the grip of this binary vice. As a contributor to one of the volumes of centenary essays concluded: 'If the critical debate is to go on effectively, the writings of Arnold cannot serve merely as a censorious road-block to the new critical approaches.'[5]

The recent vogue for cultural studies has had a rather mixed effect

[3] Tony Pinkney, 'Editorial: Towards 2000', *News From Nowhere*, 5 (1988), 9.

[4] Graham Holderness, 'Matthew Arnold: The Discourse of Criticism', in Gary Day (ed.), *The British Critical Tradition: A Re-Evaluation* (London, 1993), 29.

[5] William B. Thesing, 'Afterword', in Clinton Machann and Forrest D. Burt (eds.), *Matthew Arnold in His Time and Ours: Centenary Essays* (Charlottesville, Va., 1988), 201.

on Arnold's standing. In many respects there is nothing new in the repudiation of what is represented as the 'traditional' notion of culture. As I indicate in my final chapter, the rather narrow range of art and literature invoked by self-styled 'Arnoldians' in the first half of the twentieth century has increasingly come to be designated by the limiting, and often simply derogatory, term 'high culture'. This change has involved not just the attempt to elevate other, more popular, forms of cultural activity to a comparable level of importance and recognition with the traditionally prestigious arts; it has, more fundamentally, rested on the denial of the unitary conception of 'culture' at all. In many contexts it has become mandatory to speak of 'cultures' in the plural, with the result that any attempt to discuss the civilizing or fulfilling nature of 'culture' *tout court* is immediately liable to be castigated as an ideological imposition by special interests. Thus, the informing emphasis of 'cultural studies' in the last decade has been precisely the denial of the possibility of one, agreed 'culture' or of the confident assumptions evident in the idea of 'the best that has been thought and said'. Cultural studies has made marginality, difference, multiplicity its central theme: it sees any talk of a 'centre' as an ideological smokescreen behind which coercive conservative forces prepare to suppress challe ges to the existing orthodoxy.

It has to be said that one of the dangers of this emphasis is its inattentiveness to the rich texture of those cultural strands it regards as 'dominant'. Part of the self-dramatization that appears to be so necessary to those who see themselves as making 'radical interventions' is to represent themselves as going forth to battle against a dragon called, variously, 'the Establishment', 'the dominant culture', 'the centre', 'the élite', 'the metropolis', and so on (the choice of terms reflecting, of course, different theoretical traditions). But these are all unhelpfully objectifying labels. The 'centre' is a night in which all cows are black, virtue exclusively inhabiting peripheries. 'The ruling élite' denominates a featureless landscape of sameness, populated by privileged robots who unreflectively carry on their daily round of perpetuating dominant images, excluding marginal groups, and reproducing exploitative practices. The complexity of a culture can never be adequately depicted using such clumsy instruments.

Proponents of cultural studies urge us to be more alert to difference, but they too readily assume that the business of a 'dominant culture'/

'hegemonic power'/'ruling élite' or whatever is to suppress difference in an ideological construction which normalizes 'the centre' and demonizes or exoticizes the 'marginal'. This exaggerates both the agency and the singleness of purpose of such groups. Moreover, cultural difference is both more and less pervasive than this: more because these so-called dominant groups or cultures are themselves far from monolithic; less because the different groups and 'discourses' in a culture are never self-contained or purely oppositional, but share concepts and values and engage in constant commerce, often intelligible and profitable commerce, with their cultural neighbours, including the most powerful ones.[6]

Although Arnold continues to be identified as one of the chief sources of 'hegemonic discourse', his own engagement as a cultural critic and his constant concern with the social power of literature mean that his example is a somewhat ambivalent one for proponents of cultural studies. There is a notable difference here from attacks on him in the name of 'literary theory' in the previous couple of decades, since Deconstruction (to take the most prominent of the approaches grouped under that label) had in many ways shared with the New Criticism, the chief critical idiom it saw itself as attempting to displace, a concentration on a narrow canon of literary works and a studied removal from immediate social engagement. Arnold, by contrast, positively relished making what would now be called an 'intervention' in public debate; he was, in other words, willing to get his hands dirty. In this respect, Arnold on the iniquities of 'payment by results' in education or Arnold on the indefensible position of the Anglican Church in Ireland has more in common with the most 'committed' radical critics in either Britain or America who currently sail under the flag of 'cultural studies' than either have with, say, Cleanth Brooks on tension and ambiguity in the odes of Keats or Geoffrey Hartman on instabilities of meaning in Wordsworth.

Both these developments, as my examples suggest, have been particularly marked in the United States, though they are thereby bound to be felt, even if only in diminished form, in other parts of the English-speaking world. And even though American academic life sometimes seems to outside observers to be curiously disconnected from

[6] I have here drawn upon my 'Badly Connected: The Passionate Intensity of Cultural Studies', *Victorian Studies*, 36 (Summer 1993).

actual national and local politics, there has been an unavoidable political dimension to discussions of Arnold's relevance. For this reason if for no other, one is justified in sorting many of those who have most insistently invoked Arnold's name into two camps, the Right-Arnoldians and the Left-Arnoldians. Right-Arnoldians take a conservative view of culture as of much else: there is a cultural heritage, largely already in place and agreed upon, which it is the duty of each generation to conserve and transmit, and which has valuable civilizing and corrective functions in the present. Attempts to modify it, dilute it, or replace it with something else should be resisted: these reflect trendy progressivism, radical theorizing, self-indulgent experiment—in short, they are contemporary expressions of 'anarchy'. The canon of works of literature or art is not seen as reflecting any pattern of status or power (social, economic, or political) in the past, but rather as embodying timeless values. Arnold's style, too, is applauded as the proper civilized, even gentlemanly, manner appropriate for real lovers of culture, as opposed to all forms of barbarous technicality, over-abstraction, and jargon.

Left-Arnoldians tend rather to look to Arnold for an exemplary instance of how to bring a critical perspective to bear upon the pieties of one's own society. They recognize that many of his substantive judgements and tastes are now irretrievably dated, but they insist that his attempts to flay the philistines and tease the complacent still set the agenda for cultural criticism. Left-Arnoldians particularly celebrate the accessibility and topicality of so much of Arnold's writing, seeing in this an antidote to a withdrawn or arcane professionalism which they feel threatens the very possibility of being a social critic in the present. Among his works, they tend to prefer essays such as 'The Function of Criticism' rather than the high-toned bits of *Culture and Anarchy* or the incense-swinging of the 'Study of Poetry' essay. In other words, where Right-Arnoldians fasten above all on the notion of 'culture', Left-Arnoldians incline rather to focus on 'criticism'.[7]

I inhabit a cultural situation which makes it easier to indulge my temperamental preference for not being drawn in to such partisan

---

[7] Ideal types are never wholly instantiated by single cases, but for representative illustrations of these two composites see, respectively, Joseph Epstein, 'Matthew Arnold and the Resistance', *Commentary*, 73 (1982); and Morris Dickstein, *Double Agent: The Critic and Society* (Oxford, 1992).

side-taking exercises, but I had supposed that it would be clear from the pages of this book that I have no sympathy with the Right-Arnoldian appropriation of this particular Victorian writer to add a historical veneer to an intransigent anti-modernism. I explained in the original Preface my reasons for writing what I anticipated would strike some unsympathetic readers as a 'culpably indulgent' portrait of Arnold, but in retrospect I recognize there may have been some naïvety in not foreseeing how reductively this might be construed. In any event, alongside the generally flattering reception the book received, there was an occasional imputation of a conservative polemical purpose which I found, and find, hard to recognize, though it helped to educate me about the cultural geography of the terrain on which I had rather blithely set foot.

The year in which the first edition of this book appeared (1988) was the centenary of Arnold's death, and the events that were organized to mark the occasion provide another useful indication of Arnold's present standing and identity. In Britain two events, in particular, confirmed both Arnold's continuing prestige and, not altogether contradictorily, his capacity to serve as a whipping-boy for oddly ill-assorted antagonists. The first of these events was a series of five radio talks devoted to his work, delivered on consecutive evenings on that quintessentially Arnoldian medium, the BBC's Radio Three. The very fact that such a series of programmes was broadcast at all may be thought a sign of some deep continuities in British intellectual life, though changes in the BBC since then, and especially the replacing of talks with talking, make it unlikely that such an event will ever take place again. The tone of the talks was very far from reverential; what united the speakers was not discipular enthusiasm but rather an inclination to treat a discussion of Arnold as an apt occasion to pursue some larger controversial purpose. For example, Sir Roy Shaw, formerly Secretary-General of another organization with recognizably Arnoldian roots, the Arts Council, in what was in some ways the most sympathetic and self-effacing of the talks, did justice to the delicate balance between Arnold's genuinely democratic sympathies and his unashamedly patrician tastes. In doing so, Shaw skilfully brought out why a proper understanding of Arnold's writing would entail a critical view of what he could appropriately term the 'philistine' educational policies of the Tory Governments of the 1980s, and concluded by reaffirming that Arnold ought to be 'compulsory reading for the Secretary of State for Education and for all politicians who talk of "Victorian values" '. Unfortunately, there is precious little evidence that any of the several politicians who have been occupying that high office in recent years have been reading their Arnold. (Not, it would have to be said, that Arnold now enjoys the standing he once did among professional educationalists. Up to the 1930s and 1940s they probably provided the most constant and appreciative of his audiences, drawing direct practical inspiration from a writer who was also an inspector of schools, but those days have clearly long passed. It is perhaps indicative of this change that when Cambridge University Press first published its separate edition of *Culture and Anarchy* in 1932 it was in a series entitled 'Landmarks in the History of Education'; earlier this year the edition intended to replace it appeared in a series called 'Texts in the History of Political Thought'.)

The other centennial event was a conference whose organizers had expressed their confidence in Arnold's continuing capacity to provoke by eschewing a merely dutiful academic gathering of Arnold *Gelehrte*; instead, they invited an imaginatively chosen range of speakers to consider the fate of Arnoldian themes in the present, under the street-wise title 'Culture and its Rating at the Present Time'. Here there was abundant discussion of Arnoldian themes, but again with no merely pious or antiquarian intent—indeed, the surrounding inner-city destitution of Liverpool (the choice of venue alluded to Arnold's having died while visiting the city) was invoked more than once as a way of keeping the deliberations in perspective. And the dominant tone of the gathering was sombre and pessimistic, following the note struck by two of the main speakers: Donald Davie, eloquently giving voice to the values of provincial, Dissenting Englishness, and George Steiner, moving familiarly in the company of Freud, Nietzsche, Derrida, *et al.*, converged, despite these very different idioms, in finding Arnold and his ideals of 'culture' wanting when confronted by the problem of evil. His 'failure' they both regarded as representative of the wider failure of shallow secular humanism in the face of the great issues of eschatology. Some of the distinguished Arnold scholars present tried to propose more sympathetic or more fruitful ways of considering his legacy, but they proved powerless to dislodge Original Sin and the Holocaust.

In considering questions of religion, history, and culture, Arnold had famously insisted that we need 'the tact which letters, surely, alone can give'. Such intellectual or literary 'tact' may be no more than a second-order virtue, in danger of fading into a merely bloodless gentility unless fuelled by other passions and purposes. But a virtue it none the less can be when properly cultivated, and perhaps if Arnold had been lounging affectedly at the back of the hall he would have been unable to resist interjecting a little of that 'tact', with its sense of proportion and lightness of touch. In practice, the study of 'letters' since his time has embraced, as this gathering attested, both a form of professional expertise (here largely represented by North Americans) and the vatic utterances of the sage or cultural critic (a role apparently more readily available in Britain). Perhaps the central question not addressed at this conference was how far the connection between the two is intrinsic, as opposed to being a matter of historical contingency.

Such events, and the coverage they received in the literary press, confirm that Arnold continues to have a more than purely academic significance. Neglect is not what he currently most suffers from; rather, he is, as John P. Farrell justly observes, 'equally threatened by devoted mummification and formulaic denigration'.[8] Each of these one-eyed responses can be seen as failing to live up to the injunction to 'see the object as in itself it really is'; each is an example of what Arnold termed (in the passage cited in Chapter 1) 'the systematic judgement', the 'most worthless' of all kinds of criticism: 'Its author has not really his eye upon the professed object of criticism at all, but upon something else which he wants to prove by means of that object.' (p. 12) This point might be turned against some of Arnold's zealous champions at least as readily as against his severest detractors, and even some of his most distinguished and discerning admirers can be led to overstate their case at times. In a recent centenary contribution, R. H. Super, the doyen of Arnold studies, declared: 'If Arnold is so much more satisfying than John Stuart Mill, it is because Mill totally lacked the ability to view himself and his world from a distance.'[9] There is surely exaggeration here. For one thing, if we want to use the language of the

---

[8] Farrell, 'Writer as Touchstone', 4.

[9] R. H. Super, 'Sweetness and Lightness: Matthew Arnold's Comic Muse', in Machann and Burt (eds.), *Centenary Essays*, 194.

appetites we have to acknowledge that Mill's invariably substantial matter better deserves to be termed 'satisfying' than Arnold's literary *hors-d'œuvres variés*; Arnold often stimulates, but rarely satisfies. Furthermore, it is unjust to regard Mill as 'totally' lacking this capacity: we may think (especially with Arnold's help) that he sometimes took himself too seriously, and we may at times find the apostle of 'openmindedness' a shade too confident and dogmatic in his pronouncements. But Mill's sense of historical development and his frequent turning of a European light on the darkness of English politics and intellectual life afforded him a kind of distance. And by the same token we should be aware (as Super, it should in fairness be said, is elsewhere) of the limits on Arnold's capacity to attain an objectifying perspective. His irony, of course, constantly gives us the sense that he is viewing himself and his world from a distance, as in some ways he did, but we also (as I argue in Chapter 1) need to recognize this for the literary device it was.

Arnold's critics, as I have emphasized, have been particularly galled by the way his ironical and teasing tone suggests that he has found somewhere to stand, but somewhere which pretended it was nowhere in particular. And here we return to the question of whether any defensible and useful meaning can be given to the ideal of 'disinterestedness'. Perhaps the charge against Arnold that is now most frequently heard is what has been called his 'sublimation of political struggle into cultural judgements'.[10] To make this charge more precise and more persuasive, one would need to know whether one was being asked to accept that all cultural judgements necessarily fulfil this function, or whether this was something specific about Arnold's particular performance. (One might also wonder whether there are not times when it is appropriate to reproach some of Arnold's critics with sublimating cultural judgements into political struggle.) All the while that it is made to seem a more urgent task to unmask the limiting pre-conceptions lurking under all appeals to 'disinterestedness' than to try to arrive at the best approximation of that virtue in a world plagued by partisan over-simplifications, Arnold will continue to be the target for that kind of hostile criticism which has been described as

---

[10] Jonathan Arac, *Critical Genealogies: Historical Situations for Postmodern Literary Studies* (New York, 1987), 136.

'elaborately stepping over his corpse as a way of ritualizing its own maturity'.[11]

One of the dangers of the type of discussion I have been pursuing thus far, of course, is to exaggerate the true perception that all thinking and writing rests on presuppositions and is guided by interest into the distorting and confining obsession which insists that the cultural politics of a piece of scholarly work is necessarily the most important thing about it. Away from the clash of ignorant armies on the darkling plain of literary-political theatre, a lot of useful detailed scholarship on Arnold's writings has been quietly carried on. Details of some of the more important editions, studies, and essays are given in the appended supplementary note on further reading. I will not comment on the various contributions here, but I do want to pay, somewhat belated, respects to the work of John P. Farrell. The final chapter in his *Revolution as Tragedy: The Dilemma of the Moderate from Scott to Arnold* (a study which, though published in 1980, I unaccountably and shamingly failed to read before writing my own book) contains an excellent discussion of Arnold's response to the inescapable dilemmas thrown up by history, constantly finding himself obliged to navigate between the untenable and the regrettable. It will be clear that I find this a congenial reading, not least in its identifying Arnold's relatively minor essay on Falkland as one of the best expressions of this sensibility. A similar sympathy and perceptiveness are displayed in the three essays by Farrell in various centenary publications: ' "What I Want the Reader to See": Action and Performance in Arnold's Prose', ' "What You Feel I Share": Breaking the Dialogue of the Mind with Itself', and 'Matthew Arnold: The Writer as Touchstone', in the volumes edited, respectively, by Machann and Burt and by Miriam Allott and in the special number of *Victorian Poetry*, details of all of which are given below. Criticism of this order goes some way to allaying one's misgivings about the almost industrial scale of academic publication upon Arnold.

Future painters of Arnold's critical portrait will be able to profit from this and other good new work, but for the moment neither the recent flurry of scholarly attention nor the still greater abundance of half-informed references to him leads me to regret the distribution of

[11] Farrell, 'Writer as Touchstone', 4.

emphasis in this book. It is as a literary and cultural critic that Arnold has and, I would predict, will continue to have his greatest claim on us, for all that there will always be discerning admirers of his poetry, of his religious writing, of his educational work, and so on. Nor do I regret my decision to focus on the prose of the 1860s, a decision which, as I explain in the Introduction, produces a 'more cheerful and winning' Arnold than focusing on other periods and aspects of his writing would have done. Here I am unmoved by one reviewer's complaint that more prominence should have been given to his late literary essays, including the (in my view) over-anthologized 'The Study of Poetry'. These essays have been historically influential and must be acknowledged as such, but in the last decade of his life Arnold was preoccupied with the question of the effect, above all the moral effect, great literature can have on its readers, especially the less tutored among them. For this and other reasons, his essays of this period, as I try to illustrate in my discussion of them, do not exhibit that critical suppleness and discernment which has been the legacy of his best writing from the 1860s. However, an omission which does now seem culpable, even in such a short book, is a proper discussion of his *On the Study of Celtic Literature* and his complex relations with Ireland more generally, just as I should perhaps have devoted more space to his irritable and irritating, though far from wholly dismissive, views of America.

In general terms, however, I have to say that the central emphasis of this short study still seems to me the right or fruitful or (to use a quintessentially Arnoldian word) animating emphasis—that is, on the tone and temper of Arnold's mind, on his manner and voice, on the spirit of his writing. I hope I have made clear (I had hoped the book itself was unambiguous on this point, but being read is a chastening experience) that I have no wish to defend all of Arnold's particular judgements or tastes, still less to try to return to some more innocent state of the world that allowed those judgements to be made. Similarly, the notion of trying to 'imitate' Arnold's performance seems to me fundamentally misguided, only capable, even at its best, of yielding wilful anachronism and mannered pastiche. The root of these errors is the one Arnold himself diagnosed, writing to his brother Tom in 1864 about some remarks by J. A. Froude on Newman's *Apologia*, and I shall, again, let him have the last word: 'He makes ... the common mistake (so I think, at least) of taking as the interesting thing in a man the positive result at which he finally arrives; this does not matter much and is always more or less inadequate; what does matter, is the power and life and spirit which he develops on his way to it.'[12]

[12] Letter of 16 June 1864; quoted in Sidney Coulling, 'The Grave Tyrian and the Merry Grecian Once More', *Victorian Poetry*, 26 (1988), 19.

Supplementary Note on Further Reading

The years since this book's completion in 1987 have seen a surge in publications about Arnold. The annual bibliographies in *Victorian Studies* continue to provide a comprehensive guide; here I shall mention only a few of the more important items.

Kenneth Allott's edition of the poems will be superseded by the forthcoming Oxford English Texts edition of Arnold's *Poetical Works*, 2 vols., edited by Miriam Allott and Nicholas Shrimpton. The old Dover Wilson edition of *Culture and Anarchy* (Cambridge, 1932) has finally been replaced by *Culture and Anarchy and Other Writings*, edited by Stefan Collini (Cambridge, 1993), which includes, in addition to the corrected text of the third edition of *Culture and Anarchy* itself, the essays on 'Democracy', 'The Function of Criticism at the Present Time' and 'Equality'. While the projected edition of the complete correspondence is still pending, a useful addition is Forrest D. Burt and Clinton Machann, *Selected Letters of Matthew Arnold* (Ann Arbor, Mich., 1992), which reprints some of the best letters from the earlier collections, together with a few of those which have come to light more recently.

The centenary of Arnold's death in 1988 provoked the appearance of several major collections of essays. Miriam Allott (ed.), *Matthew Arnold: A Centennial Review* (*Essays and Studies*, vol. 41; (London, 1988) contains several good essays, especially on the poetry; Clinton Machann and Forrest D. Burt (eds.), *Matthew Arnold in his Time and Ours* (Charlottesville, Va, 1988) is more historical in focus and more variable in quality. The special centennial number of *Victorian Poetry* (vol. 26, 1988), edited by John P. Farrell and Jerold J. Savory, includes useful essays on the prose as well as the poetry; the special number of *News From Nowhere* (vol. 5, 1988) on 'Matthew Arnold and the Fate of Critical Humanism 1888–1988', edited by Tony Pinkney for 'Oxford English Limited', is primarily polemical, more illuminating of certain strands in contemporary cultural politics than it is of Arnold's writing.

Among recent monographs are David G. Riede, *Matthew Arnold and the Betrayal of Language* (Charlottesville, Va., 1988), and Mary W. Schneider, *Poetry in the Age of Democracy: The Literary Criticism of Matthew Arnold* (Kansas, 1989). Arnold's place in the world of mid- and late-Victorian intellectuals is explored in Stefan Collini, *Public Moralists: Political Thought and Intellectual Life in Britain 1850–1930* (Oxford, 1991). Numerous works illustrate Arnold's role in contemporary critical and cultural debates. For example, Morris Dickstein, *Double Agent: The Critic and Society* (Oxford, 1992) includes a shrewd appraisal of Arnold as a cultural critic, while less sympathetic accounts are to be found in Jonathan Arac, *Critical Genealogies: Historical Situations for Postmodern Literary Studies* (New York, 1987), and Gary Day (ed.), *The British Critical Tradition: A Re-Evaluation* (London, 1993).

Index

Index

Printed in the United States
135525LV00001B/15/P